AF272326

Words

of

Wisdom

Inspirational Quotes from Wise People
for Personal Growth
– And Their Interpretations

Hannu Pirilä

HP

Words of Wisdom | Hannu Pirilä

First Edition

© Hannu Pirilä/HPA Consulting Oy, 2025

Publisher: BoD · Books on Demand, Mannerheimintie 12 B, 00100 Helsinki,

bod@bod.fi

Print: Libri Plureos GmbH, Friedensallee 273, 22763 Hampuri, Saksa

ISBN: 978-952-80-9562-0

Editing: Hannu Pirilä

Images: Hannu Pirilä

Index

Introduction	1
Our Experience of Life	6
Perception	14
How Have We Created Our Lives – So Far?	20
Creating a New Life	25
Vision, Goals and Directions	29
Meaning and Purpose	35
Values And Beliefs	41
Beliefs and Fears	52
Happiness	63
Success	70
Growth and Change	76
Gratitude	87
Abundance	92
Freedom	96
Love	101
Health and Well-Being	110
Actions and Behaviors	120
Thought	135
Miscellaneous Wisdoms	139
Conclusion	145

APPENDIXES:

Acknowledgments   157

End Notes   161

Bibliography   182

About The Author   190

Other Books by Hannu Pirilä   194

Introduction

Let me start by giving you a metaphor.

Imagine living in a cave system. This cave system provides you with everything you need to survive: food, drink, work, etc.

In this cave system, you do the things you were taught in childhood and you feel your life is more or less safe. Of course, all kinds of adversities and dangers come your way from time to time, but life always goes on despite them.

In this cave system, there are countless caves and corridors, with spaces of different sizes, smaller and larger, in between, and over time you have learned to move around in the system, gradually expanding your familiar territory.

One of the challenges of living in the cave system, however, is that you can only see a very limited part of the cave system at a time as move around there with your lantern. You can never be sure what will come around the corner or the bend. You react to everything you encounter in ways that you have learned along the way.

Your life in the cave system runs itself much as a reaction to your environment, and all good and bad things come from your environment, in one way or another. Basically, you just do what you've been taught to do and hope that nothing too bad is going to happen.

However, every now and then you hear stories from other cave dwellers about a different world. In certain circles, there is a rumor that there are exits from the caves and that on the other side of them, a completely different, bright and ample world opens up. A world with unlimited possibilities!

The vast majority of the fellow cave dwellers consider this outer world to be a fairy tale, and even those who consider it possible find it quite frightening. If there are unlimited possibilities, there must also be unlimited threats!

Every now and then you hear from someone who has met someone who has been outside the cave system and some who even live there. According to them, life outside the cave system is something incredibly wonderful. Some of them also reportedly offer guidance to those who are interested in finding their way out of the caves into this bright and ample world. Some have reportedly even gone with these guides. However, few have dared. Why leave the cave system that you know? What could be so wonderful outside of it? Does such a world really exist? Why take the risk – what if I can't find my way back if I want to?

So the vast majority of cavemen would rather stay in their limited but familiar caves than go see what life outside could offer.

Our minds are like that cave system I described: restrictive, but familiar. According to Dr. David R. Hawkins, almost 80% of people live inside their minds in a world like the cave system I described. Almost 80% of people live their lives repeating the same thoughts and the same actions, achieving the same results in their lives, staying in the familiar but restrictive environment.

The wise people whose words I quote in this book are all like those guides I described, and they have dedicated their lives to help people just like you and me to come out of the metaphorical cave system and see the bright and ample world with unlimited possibilities that is outside and accessible.

With the help of these wise guides, it is my aim to do the same.

Why Me? Why This Book?

I became interested in self-development some 30 years ago because I somehow wanted to get more out of life. Slowly my interest grew as I started to realize how much I actually can influence on how I feel and how I perceive my life.

As years went by, I started to read more and more books and attend seminars and trainings. Some of the books and seminars were amazing, some not so much. For the last twenty years or so I have also collected quotes and wise words from the books I've read and the seminars and trainings I've taken.

This book contains what I think are some of the wisest and most inspiring quotes I have collected so far. My job in this book has been to choose the quotes that I think will fit best to the purposes of the book, to put them in a coherent order and to write some of my own thoughts and interpretations that I think will help in understanding them.

On the other hand, one must remember that my thoughts and interpretations are only my own perceptions; they are not the truth. It is important that you take in whatever will make you grow in the direction that is best for you.

Largely for the same reason you may find some of the quotes contradictory. They may be or they may not be. They represent the views and thoughts of different people. Although they may not be the "truth," they might still be exactly what you need to find your own way to the truth. At the very least, I believe that all the quotes in the book – as well as my own comments – will guide you towards your own personal growth.

Some quotes also contain words with strange capital letters. These words are related to the broader contexts of the books, which are not apparent from the short quotes. However, I have decided to leave these capital letters in the quotes to preserve their originality. This is just for the reader's information in advance...

Although the ultimate goal of this book is to help people grow mentally and spiritually and, thus, make this world a better place for all of us, my intention is not to try to tell you how to live your life. The main purpose of this book is to give you more motivation, inspiration and insights to find your own way to your personal growth.

Another purpose is to give credit to some of the greatest minds that I've come across so far. At the end of this book, you will find a complete list of the sources and a list of the books I have used. I highly recommend you read all of these books.

In a way, the quotes I have gathered represent the journey I have traveled in the world of self-development.

In the beginning, I read a lot of books – and collected a lot of quotes – on how to solve my problems, how to move ahead in life and how to set goals for myself. As I moved along on my path, I started to learn about the meaning our beliefs have on our thoughts and emotions, and how our thoughts affect our perceptions and how we experience life.

The more I got to understand how we truly are responsible of our lives and how we create our experience of our lives with our thoughts and perceptions, the more I became interested in the spiritual part of how we experience life.

All these stages can also be found in this book. Although these stages are somewhat scattered throughout the pages of the book, the order of the chapters is loosely following my own journey of self-development.

How to Read This Book

You can naturally read the book the way you want. There is no right or wrong way.

However, it is my recommendation that you first read it from beginning to end and once you've done that you can come back to specific chapters and topics whenever you feel like reviewing them.

By reading the book first from beginning to end will give you an overview of the journey that, according to my observations, most of us, in varying versions, go through on the path of our personal growth. I believe that might be also helpful for you in order to have the most coherent experience of the book.

Later, you can either choose to look at certain chapters or topics or simply open the book randomly to seek for inspiration whenever you feel like you could use some. Sometimes a random opening of a book will provide you with the exact thing you were looking for...

Regardless of the way you choose to read this book, I wish you rewarding and inspiring moments with it.

In Vantaa, Finland, March 2025

Hannu Pirilä

Chapter One
Our Experience of Life

What is our experience of life? How do we create that experience? What are we here for? How should we live our lives?

These are questions that many of us ponder throughout our lives. This chapter aims to provide some insights and answers to those questions.

Let's start with some general thoughts about life and some information on how we create our experience of life.

How Do We Create Our Experience of Life?

Our experience of life on Earth is shaped by a dynamic interplay of internal and external factors, involving the mind, body, environment, and our relationships with others. Here's a breakdown of how this process works:

1. Perception: Interpreting Reality

Sensory Input: We perceive the world through our five senses — visual (sight), auditory (sound), kinesthetic (tactile), gustatory (taste), and olfactory (smell). These senses provide raw data about our surroundings.

Filters of Perception: Our brains filter this sensory data through past experiences, beliefs, and cultural conditioning, among other things. Two people can experience the same event but interpret it differently based on their unique filters.

2. Thought: Constructing Meaning

<u>Internal Narratives and Images</u>: Thoughts are like the stories we tell ourselves about what is happening. They shape our understanding of events, turning raw sensory data into meaning.

<u>Beliefs and Assumptions</u>: Deep-seated beliefs influence how we think about life, shaping our expectations and interpretations of the world.

3. Emotions: Adding Depth to Experience

<u>Emotional Responses</u>: Emotions arise as a reaction to our thoughts, perceptions, and experiences. For instance, if you interpret a situation as threatening, you may feel fear.

<u>Emotional Memory</u>: Past emotional experiences influence how we respond to similar situations in the future, reinforcing patterns of feeling and reacting.

4. Action: Interacting with the World

<u>Behavioral Choices</u>: The way we act shapes our experiences. For instance, responding with curiosity versus defensiveness can create entirely different outcomes in a situation.

<u>Habits and Practices</u>: Repeated behaviors become habits, which create a framework for how we live day-to-day.

5. Environment: Shaping Context

<u>Physical Environment</u>: Where you live, your surroundings, and the people around you play a significant role in shaping your experience of life.

<u>Cultural and Social Influences</u>: Societal norms and cultural values influence how we perceive and respond to life events.

6. Awareness and Consciousness: Shaping Perception

<u>Awareness and Attention:</u> Where you focus your attention determines what you notice and how you interpret it. Practicing meditation can help you become more aware of how you're creating your experience.

<u>Choice and Intention:</u> With awareness, you can consciously choose how to respond rather than reacting automatically.

7. Meaning and Purpose: The Lens of Life

<u>Values and Goals:</u> What you value and aim for in life shapes how you experience events. For instance, someone who values personal growth might view challenges as opportunities rather than setbacks.

<u>Sense of Purpose:</u> Having a sense of meaning or purpose can color life with greater satisfaction and fulfillment.

8. The Feedback Loop: Self-Reinforcing Patterns

<u>Thought-Emotion-Action Cycle:</u> Our thoughts influence our emotions, which drive our actions, which in turn shape our experiences and reinforce our beliefs. This creates a continuous loop of experience.

<u>Neuroplasticity:</u> The brain's ability to rewire itself means that we can intentionally reshape our experiences by cultivating new thoughts, emotions, and behaviors.

We all experience, perceive, and interpret the world and its events based on our mind's proclivity to explain via mentalization and interpretations of perceived data. This process results in what is best described as the presumption that the perceived/experienced world represent 'reality'. In other words, we think that what we are perceiving is the reality when, in fact, what we perceive is our mind's interpretation – kind of its 'best guess' – of the reality.

So, our experience of life is not just about what happens to us but how we interpret, feel, and respond to those events. By cultivating self-awareness, questioning and re-shaping limiting beliefs, and intentionally focusing on growth and gratitude, we can shape a richer, more fulfilling experience of life.

"Do you know that you are the creator of your own experience?"

-Esther and Jerry Hicks [1]

"Everything we experience – joy or pain, interest or boredom – is represented in the mind as information. If we are able to control this information, we can decide what our lives will be like."

-Mihaly Csikszentmihalyi [2]

"Realize that you are the creator of your own reality. You can make choices, if you will only exercise your ability to do so."

-Bill Harris [3]

"You are the cause of all your experiences *of* life, meaning that you are the cause of your *reactions* to everything that happens to you."

-Susan Jeffers [4]

"We as human beings do not operate directly on the world. Each of us creates a representation of the world in which we live. That is, we create a map or model which we use to generate our behavior. Our representation of the world determines to a large degree what our experience of the world will be, how we will perceive the world, what choices we will see available to us as we live in the world."

-Richard Bandler and Owen Fitzpatrick [5]

"Your senses are selective – there are certain vibrations they receive and others they don't. And on top of your senses comes your noticing what your senses tell, because you don't notice everything, and that is another act of selection. Then on top of that is how you interpret what you notice – what patterns of sense you fit into it, what patterns of reason you see, and patterns of what we call 'good judgement' – and that is still another level of selection. So, the world that we are constantly aware of is a selection of your mind."

-Alan Watts [6]

"Your experience of life is primarily affected by the perspective you view it from. Depending upon the meaning we give to situations or events, we will feel and behave differently."

-Paul McKenna [7]

"Our experience of the world reflects only how we represent it to ourselves, and this is not the same as the real thing."

-Derren Brown [8)]

"This gift of imagination is a gift of power. We create our lives with our thoughts and words."

-Sandra Ingerman [9)]

"This world is your imagination. *Where your thinking is, there is your experience; As a man thinks, so is he; That which is feared is come upon me; Think and grow rich: Creative visualization for fun and profit; How to find friends by being who you are.* Your imagining doesn't change the Is one whit, doesn't affect reality at all. But we are talking about Warner Brothers world, MGM lifetimes, and every second of those are illusions and imaginations."

-Richard Bach [10)]

"All that we are is the result of all we have thought. It is founded on thought. It is based on thought."

-Buddha, *The Dhammapada* [11)]

"Once we realize that our experience of life is created from the inside-out, it follows that we each live in a unique, Thought-generated experiential reality. No two people live in the same experience of reality, and each person's reality looks real to them."

-Jamie Smart [12]

"The happiness of your life depends upon the quality of your thoughts."

-Marcus Aurelius [13]

"The world is what you think it is."

–Serge Kahili King [14]

"Remember – and this is very important – you're only one thought away from happiness, you're only one thought away from sadness. The secret lies in thought"

– Syd Banks [15]

"Until you fully understand that *you*, and no one else, create what goes on in your head, you will never be in control of your life."

-Susan Jeffers [16]

"You are the creator of your own life experience, whether you know that you are or not – so you might as well do it deliberately."

-Esther and Jerry Hicks [17]

We create our reality, and therefore our experience of life, with our thoughts, perceptions, emotions and actions, and we all have our own view of what the reality is.

By becoming more aware of your own thoughts you can become more aware of how you create your experience of life in your mind. Therefore, by changing your thoughts, you can change your life.

Next, let's have a look at what perceptions are and how they affect our experience of life.

Chapter Two

Perception

Perception is the process through which we organize, interpret, and become aware of sensory information in order to understand and interact with our environment. It involves using the five senses — visual, auditory, kinesthetic, gustatory, and olfactory — to gather data, and then processing this data in the brain, and mind, to form meaningful experiences.

The process of forming our perception begins with sensory organs receiving stimuli from the external world. Then the brain, and mind, interprets the raw sensory data, combining it with past experiences, knowledge, and context, with the aim of creating meanings to what we experience.

Out of that, we form our subjectivity: Perception varies from person to person due to differences in experiences, attention, beliefs, values, emotions, and biases, among other things.

Perception influences how we respond to stimuli and make decisions. It shapes our reality and understanding of the world. In other words, the world we experience is the perception of the ego.

In psychology and philosophy, perception is often studied to explore how individuals construct their subjective realities and the impact of cognitive processes like attention and memory on what they perceive.

Due to the subjectivity of our perception, none of us (except perhaps those who have experienced enlightenment) live in the true reality. We all create our individual outlook of reality based on our perception of the world.

"The world is real, but our perception of that world is flawed. Our mind only ruffles the surface of the reality it observes, and thus perceives only its own distorted reflection. It therefore obscures the truth of a greater Reality."

-David Perlmutter and Alberto Villoldo [1]

"All perception is based on how the brain is wired from our experiences in the past. We don't perceive things in our reality the way they are; we perceive reality the way *we* are."

-Dr. Joe Dispenza [2]

"The 'truth' is that there is no truth; there are only perceptions."

-Richard Bandler & John La Valle [3]

"Our behavior is affected by our assumptions or our perceived truths. We make decisions based on what we think we know."

-Simon Sinek [4]

"All reality is subjective...The subjective and objective are one and the same, just different descriptions from different points of perception."

-Dr. David R. Hawkins [5]

"The world is as it looks and yet it isn't. It's not as solid and real as our perception has been led to believe, but it isn't a mirage either. The world is not an illusion, as it has been said to be; it's real on the one hand, and unreal on the other...We perceive. This is a hard fact. But what we perceive is not a fact of the same kind, because we learn what to perceive."

-Carlos Castaneda [6]

"Problems don't exist independently of human beings; they don't exist in the universe at large. They exist in our perceptions and understandings. Our belief in things is what makes them real."

-Richard Bandler, Alessio Roberti & Owen Fitzpatrick [7]

"Perception does not consist of passive reception of signals but of an active interpretation of signals."

-Robert Anton Wilson [8]

"Cynical though it may at first sound, we must admit that for everyday operational purposes, truth is whatever is subjectively convincing at one's current level of perception."

-Dr. David R. Hawkins [9]

"We see the world, not as *it is*, but as *we are* – or, as we are conditioned to see it. When we open our mouths to describe what we see, we in effect describe ourselves, our perceptions, our paradigms."

-Stephen R. Covey [10]

"When we are using language as a representational system, we are creating a model of our experience. This model of the world which we create by our representational use of language is based upon our perceptions of the world."

-Richard Bandler and Owen Fitzpatrick [11]

"The changes that matter most are more often changes in perception than changes in the world outside us.

And we can change the way we perceive the world in a heartbeat."

-Paul McKenna [12]

"Desires and other worldly passions and belief systems result in selectivity of perception."

-Dr. David R. Hawkins [13]

"Certain beliefs can lead to a very bad day. *Beliefs cause stress, not your business or life situations.* It's your perception of events that cause how you feel."

—Mandy Evans [14]

"Holding on to the past also causes an inaccurate perception of the present, which can cause suffering. Perceiving ourselves, others, and the world we occupy clearly, as they really are, is the only path to happiness. And clear perception is always grounded in the present."

-Tina Turner [15]

"Your perception of any given thing, at any given moment, can influence the brain chemistry, which, in turn, affects the environment where your cells reside and controls their fate. In other words: your thoughts and perceptions have a direct and overwhelmingly significant effect on cells."

—Dr Bruce H. Lipton [16]

"Most of us acknowledge that dis-ease can be a precursor to ill health, but we can learn how to minimize those uncomfortable feelings by changing our perceptions."

-Seka Nikolic [17]

"It is a basic dictum that perception finds what it seeks."

-Dr. David R. Hawkins [18]

"Gaining different perceptions of the world is not just useful because it gives us more choices; it is useful because it makes us smarter. When you can see things in a different way, you can understand more about it, and it helps you overcome problems that once seemed insolvable."

-Richard Bandler & Owen Fitzpatrick [19]

What if you were able to change some of your perceptions? What effect would the different perceptions have on your life?

Again, since perceptions are based on our own interpretations, past experiences and the meanings we give to them, we must be capable of changing them.

How that is done is something we will explore in the coming chapters. Before we get to that, though, let's have a look at how we've created our perceptions – and therefore our lives – so far.

Chapter Three

How Have We Created Our Lives – So Far?

As you surely have become aware by now, we create our own realities, we all live in an "illusion" of the world and the life we live in.

How did that happen? How come each and every one of us lives in a "reality" that is different form anyone else's? What are the "building blocks" we have used to create our perception of life? How does it all affect how we experience life?

One of the features of our brain is that it seeks what is familiar to it. We also like being right. Because of that, we tend to strengthen the beliefs, interpretations and patterns we have learned and feel uncomfortable when information that does not fit in our perception and beliefs enters our world. Familiarity feels safe to us.

Since we like what is familiar, we tend to repeat the same thoughts and behaviors over and over again. After enough repetitions, those thoughts and behaviors become habits.

Another feature of our brain – and our mind – is that we are not using it to its full capacity. It is like if you bought the latest top-of-the-line MacBook Pro computer and you only use it to send and receive some emails every now and then, even when the computer is designed and programmed to perform extremely complicated functions. In the same way, our brain – and mind – is capable for much more than what we actually use it for. A big part of the reason is because of the limited programming that has been installed in it.

Genetics play their part in our development, and so does the environment we grow up in. As small children, we have really no saying on what "programs" are installed in us. What we do with those programs as we grow older, on the other hand, is *totally* up to us. We can change *any* of them if we want to.

But before we get to that, let's look at how our brains and minds operate and how we use them to create the realities we live in.

"It is neurologically obvious that no two brains have the same genetically-programmed hard wiring, the same imprints, the same conditioning, the same learning experiences. We are all living in separate realities. That is why communication fails so often, and misunderstandings and resentments are so common."

-Robert Anton Wilson [1]

"You are where you are and what you are because of your habits of thought.

Your thought habits are the only circumstances of your life over which you have complete control – and this is the most profound of all the facts of your life."

-Napoleon Hill [2]

"Your interpretation of reality is based upon an internal map, most of which you did not choose. You have the power to change your map if you want to."

-Bill Harris [3]

"[Some people] forget that life is not about remembering and reliving unpleasantness from their past but about going forward to look at life as the adventure it can be."

-Richard Bandler, Alessio Roberti & Owen Fitzpatrick [4]

"Your beliefs become your thoughts

Your thoughts become your words

Your words become your actions

Your actions become your habits

Your habits become your values

Your values become your destiny"

-Mahatma Gandhi [5]

"The ego/mind presumes and is convinced that its perceptions and interpretations of life experiences are the 'real' thing and therefore 'true.' It also believes by projection that other people see, think, and feel the same way, and if they do not, they are mistaken and therefore wrong. Thus, perception reinforces its hold by reification and presumptions."

-Dr. David R. Hawkins [6]

"We could say that as long as you perceive your life through the lens of the past and react to the conditions with the same neural pattern and from the same level of mind, you're headed toward a very specific, predetermined genetic destiny. In addition, what you believe about yourself, your life, and the choices you make as a result of those beliefs also keeps sending the same messages to the same genes.

...You may not be able to control all the elements in your outer world, but you can manage many aspects of your inner world. Your beliefs, your perceptions, and how you interact with your external environment have an influence on your internal environment, which is still the external environment of the cell. This means that *you* – not your preprogrammed biology – hold the keys to your genetic destiny."

-Dr. Joe Dispenza [7]

So, you have created your life, both the internal and external, with your thoughts and perceptions that are based on your beliefs, values, habits and other programming that were pretty much installed in you by your genes and, especially, your environment.

Yet, it is obvious that it is not the whole truth of it. Or how is it that, for example, siblings who have the same parents and grow up in the same environment, end up having totally different kind of characters, perceptions and lives?

There must be several variables on how we create our perceptions and lives. There must also be several ways we can make changes to our lives.

Chapter Four
Creating a New Life

Your life is your creation. If you are not satisfied with your life so far, you have the power to change it.

By altering your belief systems and other programming, you change your thoughts. When you change your thoughts, you change how you feel about things and you start to give new meanings to them, thus altering your perceptions. When the perceptions are changed, your actions and behavior changes. When you act and behave in a new way you get new results. As a result of all that, you view and experience life differently.

As I have already stated earlier, as adults, we have a choice of changing any of the programming that have been created during our childhood. In my opinion, this is when the most exciting part of our lives begins!

That is the start of the process. And once you notice that you can, in fact, make changes to your thoughts, behavior and results, you open new doors for yourself. Doors that you didn't even know existed.

"You can be whoever you choose to be."
-Richard Bandler, Alessio Roberti and Owen Fitzpatrick [1]

"Life isn't about finding yourself. Life is about creating yourself."

-George Bernard Shaw [2]

"If you don't take control of your life, someone else will."

-Paul McKenna [3]

"You can learn to be a great captain of yourself. It will take time and effort, but, honestly, no more time and effort than living a mediocre life. *It's up to you.*"

-John Assaraf [4]

"When you follow the same path everybody else is on, you get where everybody else has been. I'm giving you permission to forget all the guidelines, forget all the rules that other people have put on you, and forget what society has told you is right or wrong. Be yourself and do what makes you happy...What I am saying is, start realizing your true worth and know you can evolve in the direction you choose."

-Dean Graziosi [5]

"A great maturity opens in the human psyche when we accept that we can control our impulses by conditioning our thoughts, and that we alone are responsible for our emotions and reactions in life."

-Brendon Burchard [6]

"Act as if you are the controlling element of your life. When you do, you will be."

-Richard Bandler, Alessio Roberti & Owen Fitzpatrick [7]

"Many people flee from their freedom and refuse to live their own lives in their own way. It's just much easier to do as we are told. Then we can always blame someone else for all our problems. Taking your life into your own hands is scary. But the reward is a more valuable life."

-Frank Martela [8]

One of the major aspects of creating a new life for yourself is to not let the external world and environment run your life. If all that you do is react to what other people and media say or do, you are not in control of your life.

To take control of your life, instead of reacting, you can choose how you respond to the external stimuli; you can choose what you focus on. Do you focus on what's wrong in the world or do you focus on what you can do to make things better?

In order to create a new life for yourself, it is good to have a clear idea of what you want your life to become. You need a vision of a new life.

Once you have that vision, you can use it as the direction you want grow to.

Next, we're going to have a look at the meaning that vision, goals and direction have in the new life you want to create for yourself.

Chapter Five
Vision, Goals and Directions

Vision and goals are crucial because they provide us with **direction, purpose, and motivation**.

Vision is the big picture which you can break down to translate your desires into clear, actionable goals and directions.

Here's why they matter:

Clarity of Purpose

A <u>vision</u> acts as a guiding light, showing where you want to go. It defines your aspirations and helps prioritize what truly matters to you.

<u>Goals</u> break the vision into actionable steps, making the process more tangible and achievable.

Motivation and Inspiration

A compelling vision gives you a sense of <u>meaning</u> and fuels your passion. It reminds you why you're putting in effort, even during tough times.

Achieving smaller, incremental goals provides a sense of progress and keeps you motivated.

Alignment and Focus

A clear <u>vision</u> ensures that you stay aligned on your <u>purpose</u>, minimizing distractions.

Well-formed <u>goals</u> provide a roadmap to maintain focus, helping you concentrate on specific tasks that contribute to the vision.

Decision-Making

Having a clear <u>vision</u> and <u>goals</u> makes it easier to evaluate options and make decisions. If something doesn't align with your vision or contribute to your goals, it's easier to say no.

Measuring Success

<u>Goals</u> offer a way to measure progress and success. They help you evaluate whether you're moving closer to your <u>vision</u> or need to adjust your efforts.

Resilience and Adaptability

A strong <u>vision</u> gives you the resilience to persevere through challenges. When setbacks occur, and they will, you can adjust your <u>goals</u> without losing sight of the bigger picture.

In a way, vision provides the *"why"* — the bigger picture and long-term aspirations — while goals give you the *"how"* — the specific steps to get there. Together, they empower you to stay on track, measure progress, and achieve meaningful outcomes.

To clarify your vision, identify what you truly want: Take time to reflect on your values, passions, and goals. Ask yourself: "What kind of life makes me feel fulfilled?"

We will explore meaning, purpose and values in more detail in later chapters. Now, let's explore vision, goals and directions.

"When you make great, big goals – whether you get to them or not – the things that happen along the way are what makes life wonderful."

-Richard Bandler [1]

"Setting goals is the first step in turning the invisible into the visible – the foundation for all success in life."

-Anthony Robbins [2]

"You always get more of what you focus on in life."

-Paul McKenna [3]

"Life is a journey and it's worth checking at regular intervals that the direction is still right."

-Frank Martela [4]

"To truly build a better life, you need to make sure you're making continuous progress. You need to ensure that you're achieving the goals you set, for the person you'll become as a result of achieving them."

-Richard Bandler, Alessio Roberti & Owen Fitzpatrick [5]

"If you are predominantly thinking about the things that you desire, your life experience reflects those things. And, in the same way, if you are predominantly thinking about what you do not want, your life experience reflects those things."

-Esther and Jerry Hicks [6]

"When you focus on the outcome rather than the obstacle, your life will never be the same."

-Dean Graziosi [7]

"We are engineered as goal-seeking mechanisms. We are built that way. When we have no personal goal which we are interested in and which 'means something' to us, we are apt to 'go round in circles,' feel 'lost' and find life itself 'aimless.' People who say that life is not worthwhile are really saying that they themselves have no personal goals which are worthwhile."

–Maxwell Maltz [8]

"There are essentially only three things you need to have a wonderful life:

1. A clear direction (your Dream)
2. A well-aligned compass (your Values)
3. Milestones you can visit along the way to your ultimate destination (your Goals)

-Paul McKenna [9]

"People who find their lives meaningful usually have a goal that is challenging enough to take up all their energies, a goal that can give significance to their lives."

-Mihaly Csikszentmihalyi 10)

"If we have no worthwhile personal goals, it is easy to conclude that life itself is not worthwhile."

-Bobbe Sommer and Maxwell Maltz [11]

So, goals work as drivers for our behaviors. With goal setting comes a caveat, however.

If we let external goals drive our lives and we are constantly reaching for more and more things that are not coming from the inside of us, there is a danger that we will never be truly happy and satisfied with our lives.

There will always be nicer car, a more luxurious home or a fancier gadget on the market. If we always think that "when I get that, then I'll be truly happy," the goals are constantly moving further away from us and we will never achieve the happiness we look for. That is not what inspires for personal growth.

"Happiness is the inner psychological reward for achievement of externalized goals as a self-reward system, and the error is to think that the source of happiness is due to the 'out there' instead of originating from within."

-Dr. David R. Hawkins [12]

A vision gives a direction, and goals provide the steppingstones to a more meaningful life. Therefore, it is extremely important that you choose your goals wisely and that you check them from time to time.

There is also a difference between wanting something and desiring something. In my mind, wanting something doesn't necessarily create attachment to what we want the way desiring something does. If we are attached to a desired goal, the goal is controlling us. But if you let go of the attachment, *you* are in control of the things you want.

Another way to look at it is that if goals are not achieved within the desired timeframe, they may become stressors. Also in that case you are not really in control of your life anymore; the goals take the control. The trick again is to let go of the need and desire of what you want.

There is a reason why greed and lust are included to the seven deadly sins. To me, both indicate strong desire with attachment to something outside of us that we crave.

To ensure that you are living a fulfilling life, it is very important that you align your goals with your values, meaning and purpose. Meaning and purpose come from the inside and when your goals are coming from the inside, instead of being external desires, you will live the life *you* want, not the life you think is expected by others.

Chapter Six
Meaning and Purpose

Meaning and purpose work together with our vision and goals and are fundamental to our sense of fulfillment and well-being because they help us navigate life with clarity and resilience. Here's why they matter:

Provide a Sense of Direction

<u>Meaning</u> helps us understand *why* we do what we do, giving our actions a sense of value.

<u>Purpose</u> offers a clear path, motivating us to pursue goals and live intentionally.

Give Motivation and Energy

When we have a <u>purpose</u>, we're more likely to stay committed and persevere, even when faced with challenges.

A life filled with <u>meaning</u> feels more rewarding, making us energized to face each day.

Foster Resilience

During difficult times, <u>meaning</u> and <u>purpose</u> act as anchors, helping us to cope with stress and adversity. They also remind us of the bigger picture, giving us strength to overcome obstacles.

Enhance Mental and Emotional Well-Being

People with a sense of <u>purpose</u> report greater levels of happiness and life satisfaction. It reduces feelings of emptiness, depression, and anxiety, offering a sense of belonging and fulfillment.

Deepen Relationships

When we live with <u>meaning</u> and <u>purpose</u>, we form deeper connections with others. Shared purpose often strengthens bonds in friendships, families, and communities. It also fosters empathy and compassion, allowing us to positively impact others' lives.

Drive Growth and Contribution

<u>Purpose</u> pushes us to grow, learn, and strive for better versions of ourselves. It motivates us to contribute to something larger than ourselves, creating a sense of legacy or positive impact on the world.

Align with Values

<u>Meaning</u> and <u>purpose</u> often stem from our personal values, helping us live authentically. Acting in alignment with these values creates harmony between who we are and what we do.

<u>Meaning</u> and <u>purpose</u> are the foundations of a fulfilling life. They give us the *"why"* behind our actions and existence, the strength to overcome hardships, and the motivation to grow, contribute, and connect with others. Without them, life can feel aimless, but with them, we thrive and flourish.

Let's now explore meaning and purpose a bit closer.

"Immersing yourself in your passion is the number one way to live a truly free and fulfilling life."

-Anik Singal [1]

"If you have no purpose for your actions and no goals to pursue, you will begin to feel that your life and what you do are meaningless."

-Jari Sarasvuo [2]

"If you haven't connected with what your purpose and mission in life is, then forget anything I've said. That is the number one thing you need to do: Find out what you need to be doing on this planet, why you were put here, and what wakes you up in the mornings."

-Peter Diamandis [3]

"If you spend your day doing things that are exciting in themselves, you feel well. If you spend your time doing meaningless and frustrating activities, every morning is depressing."

-Frank Martela [4]

"I often think how terribly sad it is that so many people – the 'Thank God it's Friday' brigade – are not in the last bit passionate about what they are doing with their lives. I'm talking about the ones for whom life is all about 'making a living' as opposed to making every living moment count."

-Richard Branson [5]

"The purpose of life is a life of purpose."

–Robert Byrne [6]

"It is this spiritual freedom – which cannot be taken away
– that makes life meaningful and purposeful."

-Viktor E. Frankl [7]

"The meaning of life *is* meaning: whatever it is, wherever it
comes from, a unified purpose is what gives meaning to
life."

-Mihaly Csikszentmihalyi [8]

"The basis of life is freedom, and the result of life is
expansion – but the purpose of your life is joy."

-Esther and Jerry Hicks [9]

"The meaning of life arises from doing meaningful things
for yourself and making yourself meaningful to other
people."

-Frank Martela [10]

"Your life becomes the living miracle it is meant to be
when you free your mind to live your purpose."

-Kalliope Barlis [11)

"We're one with the universe, our purpose is to be our
magnificent selves, and the external world is only a
reflection of what's inside us."

-Anita Moorjani [12)

"Here is a test to find whether your mission on earth is
finished:

If you're alive, it isn't."

-Richard Bach [13)

Finding the purpose and meaning for your life here on planet Earth
is perhaps the main ingredient for a fulfilling life.

It is good to understand that we all can have a unique purpose, and
it doesn't necessarily have to be a "save the world" type of purpose.
Your purpose can be very small in the whole world's scale, as long as
it motivates you, is good for you and doesn't violate the well-being of
other people and our planet.

The big question, of course, is, how to find your purpose? How do
you know what your purpose is? This is a question that many of us
struggle with.

After more than 30 years of studying personal growth, I haven't found one, all-encompassing technique that works for everyone. However, I believe that finding and determining your purpose will reveal itself to you if you keep on asking that question to yourself: "What is my purpose?" And then wait for the answer.

I have found that the number one reason that prevents us from finding it is that we think of it analytically. I have noticed that the answer will not come with analytical thinking. I believe the answer will come to you when you let go of all the reasoning and contemplating, and simply let it come to you.

One thing I am sure of, however: When it comes to you it will feel exceptionally good and it will light your inner fire somehow.

> "The trick is to make everything a win/win situation. Rather than cutting up a pie, you make more pies. At one time there was no money, there were no buildings, there were no cars, there were no ideas. And look how many there are now. So basically, it must be possible to make more. Start with making more passion and excitement in your life, open your heart, and the rest will follow."
>
> -Richard Bandler & John La Valle [14]

Meaning and purpose give the basis for what you value in your everyday life. When you combine your goals with your values you will find meaning and joy in your everyday activities.

So let's have a closer look at what values actually are and how they operate.

Chapter Seven
Values and Beliefs

Our experience of life is our own creation, and we create it in our minds with our thoughts, perceptions and by the meanings we give to events in life, and to our life in general. In a way, we create our experience of life through our imaginations.

How do we choose what to create, what to imagine, then?

Some of the main components in the process are our values and beliefs that act as parts of the filtering system between the real world and how we experience it.

Values play a big part in what we give our attention to and beliefs influence on how we interpret events and things around us.

"Since we create our own reality based on our own values, our own beliefs, our own needs and our own habits, then in a sense our reality is based largely on what we imagine."
-Dan S. Bagley III and Edward J. Reese [1]

"How you perceive reality is sometimes not reality because our beliefs, values, and identity shape our thoughts – the representations we make of the world."
-Kalliope Barlis [2]

"Criteria and values are a special category of beliefs. They
are the beliefs you hold about *why* something is important
or worthwhile. They are very powerful and individualized."
-Robert Dilts, Tim Hallbom and Suzi Smith [3)]

Values

Our values are things that we hold as important to us. They are
criteria through which we sort and filter information that we process
in our minds. They determine largely what we give our focus on and
thus have a huge effect on how we create our reality.

That, what we find important defines to us, in turn, the reason why
we want to achieve a certain goal. From there also springs our
motivation to do something.

We all have also a hierarchy of values which determines what things
are most important to us and what are less important. One of the
main ways we sort and filter information, and behave, is according
to our hierarchy of values.

On the other hand, whenever we act contrary to our values, we feel
unmotivated and uncomfortable. Those feelings should be a warning
signal to us to stop and evaluate if what we are doing is in accordance
with our values and our purpose in life.

Our values also significantly influence how we make decisions. Being
clear about what we value most, makes the decision-making process
easier and faster for us.

It is worth noting that our values are not carved in stone; they change
naturally as the world around us changes and as we evolve and grow.

We can also consciously choose what we value the most and what we choose to give less importance in our life.

As your values are strongly linked with your meaning and purpose, being aware of your values can bring a lot of clarity to your life.

"How different our lives are when we really know what is deeply important to us, and, keeping that picture in mind, we manage ourselves each day."

-Stephen R. Covey [4]

"It is meaning that gives life its value, and when life loses meaning, suicide results. Meaning arises from value."

-Dr. David R. Hawkins [5]

"What are the most important things in your life right now?

Answer this question and make sure that you always have the answer clear. It will keep you aligned with your inner values. This way your decisions will always support what's most important to you."

-Richard Bandler, Alessio Roberti & Owen Fitzpatrick [6]

"If you want to make your life worth living, make choices worth living."

- Frank Martela [7]

"If you spend your days doing things that you find satisfying in themselves, you are feeling well. If you spend your time doing meaningless and frustrating activities, waking up in the morning can easily become overwhelming. If your daily activities produce results that align with your values, you are happy."

- Lauri Järvilehto [8]

"Our values are preferences."

- Dr. David R. Hawkins [9]

Beliefs

Beliefs are our perceptions and assessments of ourselves, other people, and the world around us. They determine largely what we believe to be true in our lives. However, they are not about the truth. They are about beliefs.

Beliefs are mental or psychological perceptions through which we hold something to be true or real, often without requiring concrete evidence or proof. They can be based on personal experiences, cultural influences, teachings, reasoning, or intuition, and they serve as a framework through which we interpret the world and make decisions.

Some of the characteristics of beliefs include that they are subjective, meaning that they are personal and can vary widely among individuals or cultures. They are also influential: they guide thoughts, emotions and behaviors.

Since beliefs are usually deeply ingrained in our unconscious minds, they are oftentimes resistant to change, even in the face of conflicting evidence – remember that it is our basic nature to want to be right. Even when we see clear evidence that our belief is not true and even when can see that it's downright harmful to our well-being, we often tend to hold on to our belief. That is why they can be very persistent.

Luckily beliefs can also be adaptive. Some beliefs do evolve over time based on new information or experiences.

Beliefs function in different ways. They help us make sense of the world and our place in it. They influence choices and priorities in life thus helping us in decision-making. Some beliefs can also provide hope, security, or reassurance during uncertain times.

Most of our beliefs work in the background in our unconscious mind. Many of our beliefs work in our benefit but many of them also act in a way that limits what we can do and achieve.

Once we become conscious of our beliefs and how they affect our lives, we can change them.

"Our experience of the world and life is totally the result of inner beliefs and positionalities."

- Dr. David R. Hawkins [10]

"Your quality of life is largely dictated by what you tell yourself about yourself and the world around you."

- Michael D. Yapko [11]

"Teachers like Buddha and Jesus have been telling us the same story for millennia. Now science is pointing in the same direction. It is not our genes but our beliefs that control our lives."

- Bruce H. Lipton [12]

"Any thought that you continue to think is called a *belief*. And many of your beliefs serve you extremely well: thought that harmonize with the knowledge of your Source, and thoughts that match the desires that you hold...but some of your beliefs do *not* serve you well: Thought about your own inadequacy or your unworthiness are examples of those kinds of thoughts."

- Esther and Jerry Hicks [13]

"The brain is a goal seeking mechanism...Your brain makes whatever you focus it on seem to be true in your life. This means that regardless of how much what you believe is not representative of how things really are, or how much your beliefs result in misery for you, you will arrange to be right about them by creating the circumstances that seem to confirm that what you believe is true."

- Bill Harris [14]

"We see our beliefs as truths, not ideas that we can change. If we have very strong beliefs about something, evidence to the contrary could be sitting right in front of us, but we may not see it because what we perceive is entirely different."

- Dr. Joe Dispenza [15]

"Beliefs are like blinders for humans. They can be so powerful that they cause you to see only what's in line with them. Yet they are not the truth. They are just your perception of the truth, based on your past teachings, experiences, and evaluations."

- John Assaraf [16]

"Simply put, your concept of yourself is everything that you believe to be true. And everything that you believe to be true about yourself has landed you precisely where you live and breathe every day of your life. Your beliefs about yourself are like the ingredients in a recipe that you use to create your self-concept."

- Dr. Wayne W. Dyer [17]

"*Beliefs* control behaviour and gene activity and, consequently, the unfolding of our lives."

- Bruce H. Lipton [18]

"We are living in a belief-driven world. Whatever you believe, that belief will work. It'll get you through the day, at any rate. It will frame your experiences into perceptions that make sense to you. And when something comes your way that doesn't seem to match your worldview/belief system, you'll find a way to rationalize it and force it to fit."

- Joe Vitale [19]

"We get lost by allowing our beliefs determine how we experience events."

–Owen Fitzpatrick & Alessio Roberti [20]

"The True Believer is impervious to real-world evidence because he just ignores anything that doesn't fit his belief system. Instead, he notices everything that matches and supports his beliefs, and inevitably comes to hold those beliefs at a very profound level. They can become absolutely part of his identity."

- Derren Brown [21]

"The point is that when you have a belief, even environmental and behavioral evidence won't change it because a belief isn't about reality. You have a belief in place of knowledge about reality."

- Robert Dilts [22]

"Everything we perceive is filtered through our belief and perspectives. They form the default frame for our understanding of life."

- Paul McKenna [23]

"Your beliefs limit or expand your world."

- Richard Bandler, Alessio Roberti & Owen Fitzpatrick [24]

"We humans have cognition and beliefs of all kinds, and the possession of a belief trumps all the automatic biological process and hardware, honed by evolution, that got us to this place."

- Michael S. Gazzaniga [25]

"What we experience in our lives is filtered by what we believe to be true. Our beliefs determine how we experience the universe. Thus, we never experience the world as "it is." We only experience the world as "we are.""

- Owen Fitzpatrick [26]

"It is not gene-directed hormones and neurotransmitters that control our bodies and our minds; our beliefs control our bodies and our minds, and thus our lives."

- Bruce H. Lipton [27]

"People cannot see outside of what they believe."
- Dr. Richard Bandler & Owen Fitzpatrick [28]

"A popular proverb says, "Seeing is believing," but as the philosopher Santayana once pointed out, humans are much better at believing than at seeing."
- Robert Anton Wilson [29]

"Our beliefs are at the core of our being and extremely important for our life because they guide every behavior and decision."
–Owen Fitzpatrick & Alessio Roberti [30]

"One of the most powerful ways to transform your life is to become consciously aware of your beliefs and feelings about yourself."
- Dr. John F. Demartini [31]

"You achieve what you believe. There is no variation on this truth."
- Jillian Michaels [32]

Becoming aware of those beliefs that limit you and how you want your life to be, and changing them to ones that rather empower you, will have a significant effect on transforming your experience of life.

More on beliefs also in the next chapter.

Chapter Eight
Beliefs And Fears

There are basically only a few things that are standing in the way of you living the life you want. And they are all inside of you – never in the outside world.

One reason might be that you have not yet found your purpose. If that's the case, go inside and find it. Start by doing things you love doing and follow the path of joy.

Another reason can very often be found in your belief system and fears.

Beliefs

As I have stated earlier, beliefs are our perceptions and evaluations of ourselves, other people, and the world around us.

Beliefs are important factors in our daily lives. Without them, our lives would be very difficult. Our beliefs also determine to a very large extent what we do and achieve in our lives in general.

Since beliefs are assessments and perceptions of the world around us, they also have a huge impact on what our own model of the world, our own internal map, has become.

However, a map is not the territory. This means that our *perception* of ourselves is not the same as the *reality* of ourselves and of what we are capable of. Also, our map is not the same as the reality of the world in which we live. It's just our mind's own representation of it.

By far most of our beliefs we have formed as very young children. Especially between the ages of 0-7, when our own filtering system has not yet been developed, we collect from our environment an enormous number of beliefs from other people – who also developed them mainly in their childhood.

Additionally, we make our own interpretations and generalizations about different situations. And since as children we had not yet developed any experiential base to compare things to, a strong belief may be formed out of just one experience. And once we have formed that belief in our mind, we start to make generalization of it, meaning that we generalize it to apply also on other situations because, as little kids, it helps us make sense of the world.

When you add to all that that we want to be right, we start to strengthen our beliefs very early on in our lives, making assumptions and interpretations and looking for confirmations that "prove" us that our beliefs are "truths."

It is worth remembering, however, that although our beliefs appear to us as truths, they do not represent reality.

"Everything we perceive is filtered through our belief and perspectives. They form the default frame for our understanding of life."

- Paul McKenna [1]

~ 53 ~

"I have discovered that the beliefs that have the most power over us are beliefs about ourselves that we picked up from our family at the pre-verbal age – the belief that we are not good enough or the belief that we are not lovable, for example."

-Sandra Ingerman [2]

"Whatever limiting ideas you have about yourself are not true. At some early point you took on this story, for whatever reason, and it repeated itself because you believed it to be true."

- Jillian Michaels [3]

"Whatever you believe will determine your reality."

–Owen Fitzpatrick [4]

"Humans never deal with raw experience as other animals do; they deal with experience filtered through what Dr. Timothy Leary calls a reality-tunnel and sociologists call a grid or gloss – a belief system. Every belief system (or BS) *colors* experience in a different way, rosy-red or gloomy black or some unique personal flavor."

- Robert Anton Wilson [5]

"The perceptual world is formed out of familiar forms and images held together by belief systems and energized by emotions. Whether the object or situation is loved or hated, feared or admired, seen as ugly or beautiful, depends on the observer. Such qualities do not exist in the world."

- Dr. David R. Hawkins [6]

"Whatever you believe, you will find that you are correct."
– Anita Moorjani [7]

"We have beliefs and they limit us or empower us. The kind of beliefs we have will determine what becomes possible for us."

–Owen Fitzpatrick [8]

"Most people end up having difficulties in their lives and limit how much joy they can have because the very way they think about things and the very beliefs they have prevent them from being able to achieve the best that life has to offer."

- Richard Bandler, Alessio Roberti & Owen Fitzpatrick [9]

"Your *belief* carries more power than your *reality*."
- Bruce H. Lipton [10]

"Whether you think you can or you think you can't, you're right."

–Henry Ford [11]

"That which people believe, talk about, and fear, whether it be good or bad, has a very definite way of making its appearance in one form or another."

- Napoleon Hill [12]

Fears

Fears are emotional responses to perceived threats or dangers. They arise as a natural and instinctive reaction designed to help protect us from harm, whether physical, emotional, or psychological. Fear is part of the body's "fight, flight, or freeze" response, which prepares us to deal with challenges or threats in our environment.

Fears are really based on beliefs. They are basically beliefs that something is or might be dangerous or harmful for us. And like beliefs, they are not about truths; they are our perceptions and evaluations.

Some fears are based on attachments. We are afraid that we will lose something we are emotionally attached to. If you let go of the attachment on things and people in your life, instead of *fear of loss*, you will be *free to enjoy* the possession of things and the company of people.

It is said that when we are born, we have only two fears: the fear of falling and the fear for loud noises. All the other fears we have learned somehow somewhere along the way. Therefore, basically, every fear we experience limits our lives and prevents us from realizing all the potential we really have.

"One basic truth that is of inestimable value and usefulness is the dictum that all fear is fallacious and not based on truth. Fear is overcome by walking directly into it until one breaks through to the joy that the fear is blocking. The joy that follows facing any spiritual fear comes from the discovery that it was merely an illusion without basis or reality."

- Dr. David R. Hawkins [13)]

"I'm always fond of saying that the chains of the free are only in people's minds. Your fears, your doubts, your confusions, your habits, and your compulsions are all by-products of how you're thinking, and how you're thinking dictates how you're feeling and behaving and living your life.

If you have fears, it's not that heights or spiders or meeting new people, for example, scare you; it's that you learned how to be afraid of heights, spiders, and new people. Babies are born with only two fears: the fear of falling and the fear of loud noises. All other human fears are learned. Therefore, if you learned to be afraid, you can learn to be unafraid."

- Richard Bandler [14)]

"Fear is the assumption that you're about to experience more pain than pleasure, more negative than positive, more loss than gain. Fear is an illusion that can fragment your full potential."

- Dr. John F. Demartini [15]

"If we can control our fears, we can regain control over our lives. President Franklin D. Roosevelt knew the destructive nature of fear. He chose his words carefully when he told the nation in the grips of the Great Depression and looming World War: "We have nothing to fear, but the *fear* itself." Letting go of our fears is the first step toward creating a fuller, more satisfying life."

- Bruce H. Lipton [16]

"We project our past disappointments into the future because of the fear of the unknown. In fact, we fear that the past will be recreated, so in a sense we fear what we think we know."

- Ulla Suokko [17]

"Repression is not the way to virtue. When people restrain themselves out of fear, their lives are by necessity diminished. They become rigid and defensive, and their self stops growing. Only through freely chosen discipline can life be enjoyed, and still keep within the bounds of reason."

- Mihaly Csikszentmihalyi [18)

"Personal freedom is the ability to feel what you want so that the chains of fear, sadness and hate are broken. These chains are made up of negative feelings, limiting beliefs and destructive behaviours."

- Richard Bandler, Alessio Roberti & Owen Fitzpatrick [19)

"Our most destructive fear, one that we all have to wrestle with, is the fear of change – which is, ironically, the very thing we yearn for the most."

- Jillian Michaels [20)

"People who fear can't genuinely give. They are imbued with a deep-seated sense of scarcity in the world, as if there wasn't enough to go around. Not enough love, not enough money, not enough praise, not enough attention – simply not enough. Usually fear in one area of our lives generalizes, and we become closed down and protective in many areas of our lives."

- Susan Jeffers [21)

"Few people know what it is to live without fear—but beyond fear lies joy, as the meaning and purpose of existence become transparent. Once this realization occurs, life becomes effortless and the sources of suffering dissolve; suffering is only the price we pay for our attachments."

- Dr. David R. Hawkins [22]

"What you need to understand is that fear causes the greatest damage to our health and is the root of many other negative emotions."

- Seka Nikolic [23]

"The most frequent question people ask me is why I think I got cancer. I can sum up the answer in one word: *fear*."

- Anita Moorjani [24]

"How much of your creative energy is tied up in guilt, hatred, resentment, lack, or fear? The truth is that you could be using all that energy to re-create a new destiny."

- Dr. Joe Dispenza [25]

"The more fear we have on the inside, the more our perception of the world is changed to a fearful, guarded expectancy."

- Dr. David R. Hawkins [26]

"The time you spent in fear is a distraction from living with purpose."

- Kalliope Barlis [27]

"Advice to your 30-year-old self?

'I would say to have no fear. I mean, you've got one chance here to do amazing things, and being afraid of being wrong or making a mistake or fumbling is just not how you do something of impact. You just have to be fearless.'"

-Adam Gazzaley [28]

"Confronting fears isn't always easy. No one wants to discover that the core elements of their worldview are rooted in false, fear-inspiring rules and proscriptions. But people who can confront their fears and move through them are then free to reach for their dreams."

- Bill Harris [29]

"Having a purpose provides focus, courage, and the certainty to face and break through your fears."

- Dr. John F. Demartini [30]

"Spiritually, all fear is illusion."

-David R. Hawkins [31]

Our fears are our thoughts. They are thoughts that are based on our beliefs and attachments. And as they are *our* thoughts, it is up to *us* to change them if we want to.

Think about it: what would your life be without unnecessary and limiting fears? We all are going to leave this earthly life at some point of time. What would it mean to you if you didn't have fears of losing something that you will eventually lose anyway? What would you be able to accomplish in your life if you let go of the fears? How would that change your experience of life?

Would you be happier without those fears that limit your life?

Chapter Nine
Happiness

It has been said in many instances that we all want to be happy.

What is happiness, then, and how do we obtain it?

One way of defining happiness is that it is a complex and subjective emotional state that encompasses feelings of joy, contentment, and overall well-being. It is often considered both a fleeting emotion and a more enduring state of life satisfaction. Philosophers, psychologists, and spiritual traditions have explored its meaning and sources for centuries, leading to various interpretations. Here are a few perspectives:

Aristotle believed happiness is the highest human good and is achieved through living a virtuous life. He referred to it as *eudaimonia*, which is more about flourishing and living in alignment with one's purpose than fleeting pleasure.

Epicurus viewed happiness as the absence of pain and the presence of simple pleasures, like friendship, freedom, and thoughtful living.

Existentialists, such as Sartre, focus on creating one's own meaning in life, suggesting that happiness comes from living authentically despite life's inherent challenges.

There are also different cultural and spiritual views on happiness:

In Buddhism happiness is found through inner peace, mindfulness, and detachment from desires.

In Hinduism happiness arises from self-realization and alignment with *dharma* (one's purpose).

Many of the Western religions, like Christianity, Judaism, and Islam, on the other hand, often tie happiness to faith, gratitude, and living in accordance with divine principles.

For many people, happiness is a mix of small joys (like spending time with loved ones), achieving goals, and finding purpose or meaning in life. It is dynamic and often influenced by relationships, health, environment, and mindset.

So, it seems there are many definitions and ways to achieve happiness. Ultimately, happiness is both universal and deeply personal. It might not be about being in a constant state of joy but rather about finding balance, resilience, and fulfillment in life's journey.

Many people seem to look for happiness from the external world when, in fact, true happiness comes from the inside. Happiness is a choice. If expect other people and external events to give us happiness, we are not in control of our lives and emotional states. If, instead, we choose to view the world through the positives and choose to happily do the things we do in life, we take charge of our own happiness.

The big question then is: Do we give away our power or do we reclaim the power that belongs to us?

"The source of joy is always present, always available, and not dependent on circumstances. There are only two obstacles: (1) the ignorance that it is always available and present, and (2) valuing something other than peace and joy above that peace and joy because of the secret pleasure of the payoff."

- Dr. David R. Hawkins [1]

"Happiness is only ever one thought away – but you must find for yourself that one thought!"

-Sydney Banks [2]

"If we build cheerful, happy and successful habits, we have happy, successful lives. If we're going to build grumpy, disappointed, depressing habits, we just get good at having bad feelings. Happiness is an activity: it's a skill to master."

- Richard Bandler, Alessio Roberti & Owen Fitzpatrick [3]

"Happiness is not something that happens. It is not the result of good fortune or random chance. It is not something that money can buy or power command. It does not depend on outside events, but, rather, on how we interpret them. Happiness, in fact, is a condition that must be prepared for, cultivated, and defended privately by each person. People who learn to control inner experience will be able to determine the quality of their lives, which is as close as any of us can come to being happy.

Yet we cannot reach happiness by consciously searching for it...It is by being fully involved with every detail of our lives, whether good or bad, that we find happiness, not by trying to look for it directly."

- Mihaly Csikszentmihalyi [4]

"The person who is attached to the outcome suffers if they do not get the outcome they want, whereas the happy, peaceful person prefers the outcome they want but are not attached to it. If the outcome they get is not what they wanted, they remain just as happy and peaceful as they were to begin with. Their happiness comes from within, and is not dependent on what goes on around them."

- Bill Harris [5]

"Struggle, struggle, struggle never leads to a happy ending. It defies Law. "When I get there, then I'll be happy" is not a productive mind-set because unless you are happy, you cannot get there. When you decide to first be happy – then you will get there."

- Esther and Jerry Hicks [6]

"The true source of joy and happiness is the realization of one's existence in this very moment. The source of pleasure always comes from within, even though it is occasioned by some external event or acquisition."

- Dr. David R. Hawkins [7]

"The problem with happiness is twofold. First, happiness is not achieved by striving for it. It is achieved only as a by-product of other activities. Second, no one can magically give you the keys to happiness. Happiness comes from your own life and your own choices...Happiness is based above all on a balanced and meaningful everyday life."

- Lauri Järvilehto [8]

"Happiness and freedom begin with a clear understanding of one principle – some things are within your control and some things are not."

-Epictetus [9]

"The happiness of your life depends upon the quality of your thoughts."

-Marcus Aurelius [10]

"Lasting happiness is tied to knowing who you are and what you are here to do."

- Deepak Chopra and Rudolph E. Tanzi [11]

"They live happiest who have forgiven most."

- Robert Anton Wilson [12]

"Happiness is what happens to you while you're busy doing meaningful things."

- Frank Martela [13]

"The fewer resentments you harbor, the happier your life will be."

- Robert Anton Wilson [14]

"Going back into the negative past to find happiness is like trying to make a silk purse out of a sow's ear."

- Syd Banks [15]

"By planning a life of Being Happy, you distinguish between goals and directions. When you set a direction, you include room for options, choices, possibilities and adventures. Pay attention to all the details and nothing, including you, will get lost along the way."

- Richard Bandler & Garner Thomson [16]

"**The pursuit of happiness** has become the norm, and this compulsive pursuit of making oneself happy actually reduces happiness."

- Frank Martela [17]

"When you do things from your soul,
you feel a river moving in you, a joy."

-Rumi [18]

True happiness does not come from the external world. It comes from your internal world, your thoughts. It comes from being true to yourself, living your values and purpose, being in peace with yourself. Happiness comes from the choices you make, the meaning you give to things and events. It comes from choosing your perceptions.

Funny enough, it seems that when you have found your internal peace and happiness, the external things will follow and materialize in your world, too.

Next question we're going to look at is whether success will bring us happiness? Or could it be the other way around?

Chapter Ten

Success

Success is a deeply personal and multifaceted concept that varies widely depending on individual values, goals, and perspectives. At its core, success can be understood as the achievement of goals or the fulfillment of aspirations. However, it encompasses much more than just external accomplishments or material wealth.

One dimension of success can be our personal fulfillment, feeling content and proud of our achievements and living authentically and aligning our actions with our values and passions.

It could be tied to our growth and development, continuous learning, improving, and expanding our potential, overcoming challenges and embracing change.

Some might view success in relation to our relationships, building meaningful connections with others, fostering love, and mutual respect or contributing positively to our community or the lives of others.

Success can also be defined by finding a sense of purpose and contributing to something greater than yourself, making a difference in the world, whether on a small or large scale.

To some, it could mean balance and well-being, achieving harmony between various aspects of life, such as career, health, relationships, and personal interests.

Then there are the financial and/or professional milestones, like attaining financial stability or reaching career goals or having the resources and freedom to pursue our desired lifestyle.

Success is not a one-size-fits-all concept, and its definition may evolve over time as priorities and circumstances change. Ultimately, success is about finding meaning and satisfaction in your journey while striving for the things that matter most to you.

So, success is a very personal thing. What somebody considers success for themself might not be how you rate and value your success.

This is an area, however, that can take us in a wrong direction if we are not careful. Are you trying to achieve success to become happy or are you happy to pursue success? Does the success you strive for support your values and purpose? Are you striving for success that you have defined for yourself or are you trying to fulfill somebody else's dream?

I suggest that you stop and consider what success really mean to you (personally, professionally and emotionally)?

"Success in life could be defined as the continued expansion of happiness and the progressive realization of worthy goals...Moreover, success is a journey, not a destination."

- Deepak Chopra [1]

"Success is about happy life, and a happy life is just a string of happy moments. But most people do not allow the happy moments because they are so busy trying to get a happy life."

- Esther and Jerry Hicks [2]

"The most successful people in the world are those who hold in mind the highest good of all concerned, including themselves. They know that there is a win-win solution to every problem. They are at peace with themselves, which allows them to be supportive of the potential and success of others. They do work which they love, and so they feel continually inspired and creative. They do not seek happiness; they have discovered that happiness is a by-product of doing what they love. A feeling of personal fulfillment comes naturally from their positive contribution to the lives of others, including family, friends, groups, and the world at large."

- Dr. David R. Hawkins [3]

"If one advances confidently in the direction of his dreams, and endeavors to live the life which he has imagined, he will meet with a success unexpected in the common hours."

-Henry David Thoreau [4]

"The drive to win is not, per se, a bad thing. Problems arise, however, when the metric becomes the only measure of success, when what you achieve is no longer tied to WHY you set out to achieve it in the first place."

-Simon Sinek [5]

"Success isn't about what you *have* – it's about how you *feel*."

– Jack Canfield [6]

"When success is defined by externals – money, possessions, status, and power – it's granted to the few, who usually begin from a privileged background. But what if success is defined differently, as an inner state of fulfilment? If you turn within, you can be successful at this very moment, because success is a creative process. You are engaged in it already, because true success is something we live. It's not an end state we arrive at."

- Deepak Chopra and Rudolph E. Tanzi [7]

"To be successful, you must find peace of mind, acquire the material needs of life, and, above all, attain *happiness*."

- Napoleon Hill [8]

"True Success enlivens and supports the spirit; it has not to do with isolated attainments, but being successful as a total person, attaining a successful lifestyle that benefits not only yourself but everyone around you."

- Dr. David R. Hawkins [9]

"The power of authenticity is your ticket to success, the key to fulfilment, and the investment required is that of being courageous enough to peel off your mask and bravely show up as exactly who you are."

- Jessica Huie [10]

"The standard of success in life is not the things or the money – the standard of success is absolutely the amount of joy you feel."

- Esther and Jerry Hicks [11]

"If you carefully consider what you wanted to be said of you in the funeral experience, you will find *your* definition of success."

- Stephen R. Covey [12]

"We were raised to think that failure is bad. But truthfully, failure is the cornerstone of success."

- Dean Graziosi [13]

"I have learned more from my failures than my success."

– Richard Branson [14]

"Out of defeat comes victory; out of failure, success; and out of humbling, true self-esteem."

- Dr. David R. Hawkins [15]

In many cases, success is followed by a series of "failures." When you fearlessly strive for the things you want in life and when the things you want are in line with your values and purpose, I believe you will experience a string of successes – even way before you achieve what you strive for.

Regardless of what your goals are, whatever you strive for, some kind of growth will be required. It also means that something in your life needs to change. And those are the things we're going to look at next.

Chapter Eleven
Growth And Change

To experience growth in life, we need to change the way we think.

How can we change our thinking, then?

The first thing is to have a clear idea of what or who you want to become, what is the ultimate goal of the desired change. Most people know what they want to get rid of or move away from – whether it's excess weight, smoking, stressful job, for example – but they fail to define what they want instead, what they want to move towards to.

We have already addressed goals, values and purpose in earlier chapters, so what else do we need to do to enable growth and change? Here are some tips:

Learn continuously and educate yourself: read books, take courses, and seek out experiences that broaden your knowledge and skills.

Adapt to change: stay flexible and curious and adjust your plans when circumstances shift.

Reflect regularly: periodically review your progress and refine your goals.

Let go of things that don't serve you: thoughts and beliefs that limit you, old ways of doing things, old paradigms, items that you don't use anymore...

By doing the same things in the same way, you can only achieve the same results. If you want something in your life to change, you have to do something in a new way. If you want to do something in a new way, it also requires a change in your thinking.

Life change is possible. Many have succeeded. And it doesn't even have to be painful. Sure, giving up old habits can cause some pain, but when the change you want is really good for you, the reward that comes with the change should in the end be greater than the pain of giving up the old. Also, once you get that process going, it will become easier and easier if you just keep on growing and doing what is good for you.

"The wise man changes his mind; the fool never. There can be no progress without change, no growth without renewal."

- Raymond Holliwell [1]

"As is commonly observed, growth, both individual and collective, can take place either slowly or suddenly. It is not limited by restraints, but by tendencies. Innumerable options are open to everyone all the time, because people want the context that would make them attractive. One's range of choice is ordinarily limited by one's vision."

- Dr. David R. Hawkins [2]

"When we change jobs, end a relationship, move into a new house, graduate from school, or launch into a new time of life, we are experiencing "little deaths." It is through such deaths that change happens; it is through the death of the old that something new can be born. Death and change are not something to fear for they allow the birth of the new. By learning how to gracefully let go of the old and accept change, life can become the adventure it was intended to be."

-Sandra Ingerman [3]

"Often a moment of crises, no matter how small, is exactly the point at which we begin to see things in a new way. Something is lost, but new possibilities appear... The crises doesn't have to be a national or global event; it can be quite personal and internal. It turns out that crises can be – and often is – a positive change agent."

- Bill Harris [4]

"People who stop studying merely because they have finished school are forever hopelessly doomed to mediocrity, no matter what their calling. The way of success is the way of continuous pursuit of knowledge."

- Napoleon Hill [5]

"Change happens all the time – it's the only constant in life. The point is, are you going to *choose* the direction your life will take and the kind of person you will become, or will you just sit back and wait for life to happen to you?"

- Richard Bandler, Alessio Roberti & Owen Fitzpatrick [6]

"The goal of education is "personal development"
(Swedish Law for Higher Education Section 2).

It means that knowledge is not enough. The important
thing is a positive change in our way of thinking, reacting,
doing things, etc."

- Lars-Eric Uneståhl [7]

"For you to truly make changes in your life, you would
have to step into the unknown – and if you don't, nothing
ever really changes."

- Dr. Joe Dispenza [8]

"We all think and we all believe – and once you realize
that you can alter your thinking and beliefs, it changes the
way you behave.

Beliefs aren't about truth. Beliefs are about believing.
They're guides for our behavior."

- Richard Bandler [9]

"Growth is based on someone daring to try more than
they are or can do."

- Jari Sarasvuo [10]

"Live as you were to die tomorrow. Learn as if you were to live forever."

-Mahatma Gandhi [11]

"Managers often ask me how much time they should spend training and developing their employees. My answer is always the same: 'A lot'."

- Lee Cockerell [12]

"Change your thoughts and you change your world."

–Norman Vincent Peale [13]

"It is not possible to stand still or be stuck, because Energy, and therefore life, is always in motion. Things are always changing."

- Esther and Jerry Hicks [14]

"Things do not stay the same. If you are not moving forward, they get worse."

- Richard Bandler & Garner Thomson [15]

"When you follow your inspirations and intuition, you grow in self-worth and potential, as well as toward your true capabilities."

- Dr. John F. Demartini [16]

"The only thing between you and the life of your dreams isn't you – it's the idea that you need to change..."

- Michael Neill [17]

"Change your thoughts, and you change your destiny."

- Joseph Murphy [18]

"Life without growth is rotting. When you stop pushing your limits, you begin to rot, to die away. If you don't want to grow, you will also dim the flame of those around you before your final extinction. But as long as you grow, there are more blessings ahead than you can possibly hold in your arms."

- Jari Sarasvuo [19]

"When people change what they believe in, they can change their lives."

- Richard Bandler [20]

Letting Go

By letting go of those things, thoughts, beliefs and behavioral patterns that no longer serve you, you free up space and capacity of your mind to focus on the things you want more in your life.

By letting go of negative thoughts and feelings, you will be able to invite new, positive thoughts and feelings into your life. By letting go of limiting beliefs, you allow new, more empowering beliefs to guide your life. By letting go of unhealthy relationships, you allow new, healthy relationships to enter your life.

For you to grow, you need to let go of things that are stopping you from growing. This means, oftentimes, that you need to let go of anything that causes you pain or suffering and, especially, you need to let go of your ego and its need to be right.

In my opinion, letting go of the old is a vital, yet oftentimes the hardest, part of personal growth.

"You know why it's hard to be happy – it's because we refuse to LET GO of the things that make us sad."

-Lupytha Hermin [21]

"What we are holding inside colors our world. If we let go of guilt, we will see innocence; however, a guilt-ridden person will see only evil."

- Dr. David R. Hawkins [22]

"By letting go of any negative self-judgement, we allow our world to transform; and as it does so, we'll be able to feel greater and greater trust. The more we're able to trust, the more we're able to let go of trying to control the outcome. When we try to move with this flow rather than adhere dogmatically to the doctrines of others or the beliefs we once had that no longer serve us, we more accurately reflect who and what we truly are."

- Anita Moorjani [23)]

"It's about letting go of problems and thinking more about solutions. It's about feeling good most of the time. It's about dealing with the tough times you have and the difficult people you meet with grace and skill. You have more control over your life than you think."

- Richard Bandler, Alessio Roberti & Owen Fitzpatrick [24)]

"How do we become connected with our most authentic selves? We must first learn to **let go** of who we think we should be, who other people expect us to be and who we once were. Only then can we uncover who we really are now."

- Roxie Nafousi [25)]

"I've found that letting go of stuff, not trying to push it, allows life and opportunity to come to you...Life's like that.

Don't try to force it; just let go and those doors will open for you."

– Alexander Millar [26]

"We learn that the answer to the problems we face is *within* us. By letting go of the inner blocks to it, the truth of our inner Self shines forth and the path to peace is revealed."

-Fran Grace [27]

"When you let go of a very specific outcome, the heavy weight of expectation comes off of your shoulders. You will become a different person immediately, and your happiness will skyrocket."

- Dean Graziosi [28]

"Letting go is a necessary, if sometimes heart-wrenching, gateway to genuine transformation."

- Phil Jackson and Hugh Delehanty [29]

"Willingness

This is the keystone to all spiritual progress as well as success in the world. It means letting go of resistance and finding the joy of going one hundred and one percent.

Unpleasantness is due to resistance, and when resistance is let go, it is replaced by feelings of strength, confidence, and joy."

-Dr. David R. Hawkins [30]

"I have trusted people who have fucked me and my family over, lied about me… all the horrible shit. At some point, you have to let it go or it will eat you alive and THEY win. I let them go. I am free from the haters because I took their power away. I stopped reading about myself because so many fucked-named people were trying to click-bait me into a shit-throwing contest. I fell for it a few times. I so dearly wish I had not."

- Steve Lukather [31]

"As you release the clutter from your life, your energy actually becomes lighter."

- Anita Moorjani [32]

Our brain likes what is familiar. It is also our nature to want to be right.

But those things are exactly what is preventing you from growing and reaching your full potential.

By letting go of the need to be right you open the door for new learnings to enter your life. By letting go of that feels familiar and safe – which, by the way, is merely an illusion – you allow yourself to grow in ways you thought were not possible.

Letting go is the key to make impossible possible.

Another door opener is gratitude.

What is it and why is it such an important part of personal growth, is the topic of the next chapter.

Chapter Twelve
Gratitude

Gratitude is a deep sense of appreciation or thankfulness for the things, people, or experiences in your life. It involves recognizing and acknowledging the value of what you have, regardless of external circumstances. Gratitude often shifts your focus from what you lack to what you already possess, fostering positive emotions and an improved perspective on life.

Psychologically and emotionally, gratitude has been linked to improved mental health, better relationships, reduced stress, unconditional love and a greater sense of overall well-being. It encourages mindfulness and helps people cultivate a sense of abundance rather than scarcity.

Gratitude is also about appreciating the journey, not just the destination. It's about being successful before you have achieved goal.

Gratitude can also act as an antidote for anxiety and many other negative emotions. Gratitude is about appreciation instead of lack of something.

"Gratitude is the key that opens the gateway of the heart and allows the unified field theory of love to fill your life. Gratitude makes you *present* with whatever you're doing."
- Dr. John F. Demartini [1]

"Not one day of our life will be repeated. Each day we can choose happiness, we can choose to live by our values and we can choose to be grateful for the amazing possibilities we are given."

- Paul McKenna [2]

"To live in 'an attitude of gratitude', we must cultivate it so that it becomes part of our essence. We must practice it over and over again in order to begin to rewire our neurological pathways so that we automatically focus on all the good in our lives rather than the bad."

- Roxie Nafousi [3]

"The struggle ends when the gratitude begins."

-Neale Donald Walsch [4]

"Every time we're grateful for the extraordinary architectural creation called our being, our body, and our life, we take another step toward manifesting our greatest potential and fulfilling our true and ingenious destiny on this planet."

- Dr. John F. Demartini [5]

"When you learn to change your focus, it helps you feel gratitude for what you already have – and that is truly the key to happiness."

–Anthony Robbins [6]

"When you know that bad things aren't so terrible and good things aren't so terrific, you can be quietly grateful for whatever occurs. Balance is neither pessimism nor optimism. It doesn't lean to one side or the other, but sits poised in the middle. It is "gratefulism," and that is both wisdom and true power. All things are balanced, and when you know it, you remain true to yourself rather than being driven by your hopes and fears."

- Dr. John F. Demartini [7]

"A grateful heart is a magnet for miracles."

- Roxie Nafousi [8]

"Gratitude is the key to growth and fulfillment."

- Dr. John F. Demartini [9]

Gratitude is a powerful tool for personal growth because it shifts your mindset from focusing on what's lacking to appreciating what you have.

Gratitude also means that you let go of thoughts and feelings like shame, guilt, blame, grief, fear, anger, hate, scorn and pride and view any event and experience attached to those feelings as a welcomed learning experience and gratitude.

For example, instead of feeling grief or sadness because you have lost someone, you can choose to be grateful that your paths have crossed and that you got to know that person and spend time with them.

In the same way, whenever you encounter adversity, instead of feeling frustrated or angry, you can choose to be grateful for the opportunity to learn and grow.

All that is required is a change in perception. It is all just a thought away from what you have thought, felt and done before.

Oftentimes, in order to feel gratitude, you also first need to learn how to forgive, and not only to other people. Sometimes the most difficult part of forgiveness is to forgive ourselves. We all make mistakes, and we all do stupid things. They are a part of our growth process. Take the learnings, forgive, and move on with your life.

With some practice, you can shift your mindset from lack to gratitude. To do that, some people find it helpful to keep a gratitude Journal. That can be done, for example, by writing down three things you're grateful for every day. They can be small (a warm cup of coffee) or big (a supportive friend).

Another way could be by reflecting on the positives: Before going to sleep, take a moment to think about what went well in your day and what can you be grateful for. Also in the morning before getting up, think about something you can look forward to today and be thankful for it.

Some people also use gratitude affirmations by saying things like, *"I am grateful for today's opportunities"* or *"I appreciate the people in my life."* This rewires your brain for positivity.

However you choose to do to practice gratitude, I am pretty sure you that within a relatively short time you will notice a shift in how you feel and go about during your day.

Gratitude also changes your mindset from lack to appreciating what you already have and what is going well in your life. It changes your mindset from lack to abundance, which is the topic of our next chapter.

Chapter Thirteen
Abundance

Abundance can be described as the state of having a large amount of something or having all needs fulfilled. It refers to plenty, prosperity, or overflowing supply.

For example, the nature offers an abundance of beauty and in personal abundance it can mean having wealth, happiness, or fulfillment in life.

In essence, abundance reflects a state of plentifulness or prosperity and it is something that most people wish for – in one way or another – in their lifetime.

However, many of us have been taught that aiming for wealth or abundance in life is bad or selfish. Is it really? If you don't violate the life or rights of others, what is so bad about it? Also, if you *create* abundance, instead of gathering it, you are not taking anything away from others. That can also be seen as spreading abundance.

It is said that the universe is infinitely abundant. What if you tapped into that infinite abundance and just attracted more of it to you? How would that be bad in any way?

The thing about abundance is that it, too, is first created in our minds with our thoughts.

"The basic rule of the psychic universe is that "like attracts like... This phenomenon explains many scriptural quotations and common sayings that have puzzled the intellect, such as, "The rich get richer and the poor get poorer," and "those who have, get." As a general rule, therefore, people who are carrying the consciousness of apathy bring poverty circumstances into their lives, and those with a prosperity consciousness bring abundance into their lives."

- Dr. David R. Hawkins [1]

"When we consciously choose to think positive and empowering thoughts that trigger high-vibe emotions (such as confidence, enthusiasm and hope), we will attract more abundance into our lives through the law of attraction."

- Roxie Nafousi [2]

"To bring anything into your life, imagine that it's already there."

- Richard Bach [3]

"A positive attitude isn't always looking at the glass as full and it isn't always about looking at the glass as half full or half empty. It's asking the question, where are all the other glasses?"

–Richard Bandler [4]

"You can't be sick enough to help the sick or poor enough to help the poor. You help by choosing health, prosperity, love, joy, and flow. You help by being clear, centered, and focused and learning to love, honor, and accept yourself."

- Ulla Suokko [5]

"We don't create abundance.
Abundance is always present.
We create limitation."

-Arnold Patent [6]

"Once you begin to cultivate and practice self-love, your ability to manifest will become infinitely more powerful. Self-love empowers you to step into your light, to step into your greatness and to open up space for abundance to enter your life. Self-love tells the universe, 'I am worthy of love, I deserve success, I am ready to live my dreams, and then, this is what you shall receive."

- Roxie Nafousi [7]

"Peculiarly, the unconscious will allow us to have only what we think we deserve. The more we hang on to our negativity and the small self-image that results, the less we think we deserve, and we unconsciously deny ourselves the abundance which flows so easily to others. That is the reason for the saying, "The poor get poorer and the rich get richer." If we have a small view of ourselves, then what we deserve is poverty, and our unconscious will see to it we have that actuality. As we relinquish our smallness and revalidate our own inner innocence, and as we let go of resisting our generosity, openness, trust, lovingness, and faith, then the unconscious will automatically start arranging life circumstances so that abundance begins to flow into our life."

- Dr. David R. Hawkins [8]

Abundance is available to all of us. What prevent so many of us from experiencing it are, again, our thoughts.

If the focus of our thoughts is on the lack of things – be it the lack of love, the lack of money, the lack of joy – that's what we tend to draw more to our lives.

If, instead, you pay attention to what you already have and what is available to you, your mind starts to look for ways to have more of those things in your life. Focusing on the lack doesn't give your brain the guidance out of it. Focusing on the abundance gives your brain ideas on how to find ways toward more of it.

With true abundance also comes more freedom, the topic of our next chapter.

Chapter Fourteen

Freedom

By freedom, I really mean here the personal freedom which refers, among some other things, to an individual's ability to make choices and decisions about their life without undue interference or constraints from external forces, such as government, societal norms, or other people.

The general perception is that personal freedom encompasses the capacity to act in ways that align with one's values, beliefs, and desires, while respecting the freedoms and rights of others.

According to the same perception, some of the key aspects of personal freedom include things like autonomy and the ability to govern oneself and make independent decisions. It also includes a freedom of thought and expression by having the right to hold and share opinions, beliefs, and ideas without fear of censorship or retaliation.

To many, personal freedom means the ability to travel and reside where one chooses and the freedom for privacy and the right to personal space, information, and life without unwarranted intrusion.

Another form of personal freedom is the freedom of choice: The ability to choose one's lifestyle, career, relationships, and beliefs.

It should be noted that with this type of freedom also comes the responsibility to ensure that exercising one's rights does not infringe upon the rights of others.

In essence, personal freedom means that you are not at the mercy of your surroundings but, instead, you are in charge of how you react and respond to any stimuli from your environment. That, of course, means that you are in control of your thoughts and emotional states.

In my opinion, personal freedom also means freedom form limiting beliefs and fears, and freedom from the chains of the past.

Therefore, personal freedom ultimately means freedom to choose one's own thoughts and freedom from the chackles of limiting programs of the past.

"Personal freedom is the ability to feel what you want so that the chains of fear, sadness and hate are broken. These chains are made up of negative feelings, limiting beliefs and destructive behaviours."
- Richard Bandler, Alessio Roberti & Owen Fitzpatrick [1]

"*Freedom* is the basis of that which you are because everything that comes to you comes in response to the thoughts you think – and no one has control over the thoughts that you think other than you. When *joy* is your dominant quest so that you gently train your thoughts into alignment with *who-you-really-are*, all resistance subsides, and you then allow the *expansion* or *growth* that your life experience has inspired within you."
- Esther and Jerry Hicks [2]

"Everything can be taken from a man but one thing: the last of the human freedoms – to choose one's attitude in any given set of circumstances, to choose one's own way."

- Viktor E. Frankl [3]

"The liberation of the mind is a very simple step to take. The reason many don't take it is because it must be taken over and over again many times for it to become a habit.

The liberation of your mind comes from the following principle: reality always depends on how you perceive it. Learn to perceive it more usefully and your world will transform."

- Owen Fitzpatrick [4]

"The truly important learning is to be able to do the thing you already *know* in another way. The more ways you have to do the things you know, the freer is your choice. And the freer your choice, the more you're a human being."

- Moshe Feldenkrais [5]

"Forces beyond your control can take away everything you possess except one thing, your freedom to choose how you will respond to the situation. You cannot control what happens to you in life, but you can always control what you will feel and do about what happens to you."

–Harold S. Kushner [6]

"Replacing delusions with clarity, replacing negative messages with positive ones, is the way we can free ourselves from suffering."

- Tina Turner [7]

"This is why we seek personal growth – to be *free* from the pain we cause ourselves, to make better choices, to feel better about who we are becoming, to act more confidently in social situations, and to unleash our full creativity and contributions into the world in order to make our highest difference. Gaining Personal Freedom in this sense is letting go of any self-doubt and self-loathing and allowing ourselves permission to be our unique, powerful, authentic selves."

- Brendon Burchard [8]

"Pain is part of life but suffering is optional."

- Alberto Villodo [9]

"Without the exercise of choice, no progression will occur."

- Dr. David R. Hawkins [10]

"No liberation is complete until you realize that your perceptions are your own cause, and it's up to you to empower yourself...You *are* the author of your own life."

- Dr. John F. Demartini [11]

"The best protection, so to speak, is love and freedom."

– Heiko Wenig [12]

To me, true personal freedom requires that we let go of the things that don't serve us. When you break the shackles that prevent you from becoming who you truly can be, you move towards freedom.

What has prevented you from doing that lie all inside you. The greatest obstacles on your journey to freedom are your own thoughts. And as you already know, you can change your thoughts if you want to.

After gratitude, abundance and freedom it is time to explore another significant and life altering aspect of personal growth. And that is love.

Chapter Fifteen

Love

Generally, when people talk about love, they talk about love that is somehow conditional. Some say that that kind of love is not love at all. They say that true love is always unconditional.

The primary difference between conditional and unconditional love lies in the presence or absence of conditions or expectations.

Love, as most people understand it, is a deep feeling of affection, care, and attachment to someone. It often comes with conditions or expectations. For example, people may love others because of specific traits, behaviors, or what they bring into their lives (e.g., companionship, support, shared values).

When expectations aren't met, love may weaken, fade, or turn into disappointment or resentment.

This kind of love is common in many types of relationships, such as romantic love, friendships, or familial connections. People also often confuse infatuation and love.

Unconditional love, on the other hand, is absolute and unchanging, regardless of circumstances.

It is not dependent on the person's actions, achievements, or fulfillment of expectations. This love persists even when the person you love makes mistakes, changes, or falls short of your expectations. It is selfless, compassionate, and accepting of the other person as they are, flaws and all.

This is often considered the highest form of love, it is typically associated with parental love, spiritual love, or deeply committed relationships.

The transition from conditional love to unconditional love requires that we let go of the needs and vanities of the ego and surrender to love that seeks no return or gain.

This also applies to ourselves. It is said that we cannot give love to others unless we love ourselves first. This self-love is not the same as selfishness, though. It is, among other things, about caring for yourself enough to accept all your failures and shortcomings. It is about forgiving yourself and nurturing yourself so you can grow and become the best version of yourself. It is about moving on without self-blame or self-deprecation.

In summary, one can say that love is a spectrum of feelings that can be conditional or unconditional, but unconditional love represents a pure, unwavering acceptance and commitment to someone or something, no matter what.

"Love is a neutral energy that accepts you as you are. No conditions, no judgment, no good or bad. No reward or punishment. You don't have to "try" to be worth it. It is always there for you. It receives you with open arms every time, all the time."

- Ulla Suokko [1]

"It takes both positive and negative particles in perfect synthesis to create light, and in exactly same way, you need both sides of every event to hone in on your true nature, which is also light. The light in the center is unconditional love; the emotional or particle waves are conditional love."

- Dr. John F. Demartini [2]

"True love is pure spirit power being manifest. The manifestation can take many forms. There is a mother loving her child, a doctor caring for his patient, a father playing with his children, a child with a new puppy, people caring for the less fortunate.

Love is a positive *feeling* and if people cultivate this feeling in their lives, they will surely free themselves from any unbalanced conditions that surround them.

Love is not just an idea. Love is a living, breathing essence that the wise can pluck from the air at will and then like a master artist mold it into something beautiful.

Love makes the impossible, possible."

- Syd Banks [3]

"Love is misunderstood to be an emotion; actually, it is a state of awareness, a way of being in the world, a way of seeing oneself and others."

- Dr. David R. Hawkins [4]

"The Universe is neutral. It is pure consciousness, which means it doesn't judge or evaluate. It doesn't blame or punish. The Universe is neutral in the same way love is neutral. Not the conditional love of human drama, but the pure, unconditional, divine love. It just loves everything. It supports everything. In other words, the Universe always says yes. Love always says yes. Your responsibility is to choose what the Universe says yes to."

- Ulla Suokko [5]

"Selfishness comes from too little self-love, not too much, as we compensate for our lack. . . Our world suffers from too little self-love and too much judgement, insecurity, fear, and mistrust. If we all cared about ourselves more, most of these ills would disappear."

- Anita Moorjani [6]

"There is no greater gift we can give to ourselves than the gift of unconditional self-love."

- Roxie Nafousi [7]

"What good comes from complaints? Grumbling only brings you down. Find a way forward, smile, shake it off, love yourself. Use your challenges to become stronger. This is how you can transform your karma and open your heart."

- Tina Turner [8]

"Authentic self-love is necessary for you to be able to reclaim your authentic power and to love others or the world. Only through loving yourself will you be able to receive and feel worthy. Self-love is the basis for the balance, harmony, peace, and freedom you need to live your purpose."

- Ulla Suokko [9]

"When it comes to finding the right path, there's a different answer for each person. The only universal solution I have is to love yourself unconditionally and be yourself fearlessly!"

- Anita Moorjani [10]

"Once you begin to cultivate and practice self-love, your ability to manifest will become infinitely more powerful. Self-love empowers you to step into your light, to step into your greatness and to open up space for abundance to enter your life. Self-love tells the universe, 'I am worthy of love, I deserve success, I am ready to live my dreams, and then, this is what you shall receive."

- Roxie Nafousi [11]

"When we peel off the layers produced by fear, self-love begins to shine through. Self-love is not vain. It's not selfish. In fact, it's the most selfless thing that you can do for yourself and everyone else. We can feel love for ourselves more deeply when our lives are less cluttered, when we're not preoccupied with doing things out of obligation, out of fear of disappointing or displeasing others, or out of fear of failure. Self-love is the most amazing state to be in, and the absolute best gift to yourself. You'll feel a lightness, greater clarity, and reduced or eliminated senses of fear, anxiety, and stress. Self-love increases your trust and your faith in the Universe and in your own body's ability to heal and grow on all levels."

- Anita Moorjani [12)]

"We're not here to be right, we're here to be love."

- Dr. John F. Demartini [13)]

"Freedom is everything. And love is all the rest."

- Dr. Richard Bandler [14)]

"Self-love is, at its core, allowing yourself to be a channel for the divine to express itself through you."

- Anita Moorjani [15)]

"The greatest thing I learned from my journey to the other side is that all we must do is love ourselves."

- Anita Moorjani [16]

"A truly 'normal' state of consciousness is one that is free of all negativity and instead filled with joy and love. Anything else is based on illusion and perceptual distortions."

- Dr. David R. Hawkins [17]

"It takes a number of critical factors to win an NBA championship, including the right mix of talent, creativity, intelligence, toughness, and, of course, luck. But if a team doesn't have the most essential ingredient – love – none of those other factors matter."

- Phil Jackson and Hugh Delehanty [18]

"Success is not the key to happiness. Happiness is the key to success. If you love what you are doing, you will be successful."

- Albert Schweitzer [19]

"Hell is not a condition imposed by a judgmental God, but rather the inevitable consequence of one's own decisions.

Hell is the final outcome of constantly choosing the negative and thus isolating oneself from love and truth."

- Dr. David R. Hawkins [20]

"Day-to-day problems never seem as big when viewed through a veil of humor and love."

- Anita Moorjani [21]

"The only real purpose of a goal is to inspire you to fall more deeply in love with life."

– Unknown [22]

In today's world, most people seem to be judgmental of themselves and others.

Ask yourself, what good does that bring to your life? How would your life be if you let go of judging yourself and others and replaced it with unconditional love?

Just like with gratitude, unconditional love requires forgiveness. Without letting go of all hatred, guilt and shame, unconditional love won't be possible. Forgiveness frees you up and opens the door for love.

I know it probably won't happen overnight, but if we all took even little, tiny steps in that direction, I believe it would have a huge impact on the world.

Even if you can't quite grasp the thought of what impact those things have on the world we all live in, are you aware what they can do for your own health and well-being?

Turn the page and you will find out.

Chapter Sixteen
Health and Well-Being

There are many ways we can influence our health and well-being: We can take care of our bodies by exercising, eating healthy, and getting enough sleep. We can manage our stress by practicing mindfulness, meditation, or other relaxation techniques. We can balance work and rest and avoid burnout by changing our perceptions and scheduling downtime.

As you know by now, all our actions start with our thoughts. Before you do anything, there is a thought behind the action, whether a conscious or an unconscious one.

So, whether you decide to exercise or to lounge on the couch, to eat salad or cheesecake, stress about something or relax, it all starts with your thoughts. Your thoughts create your mental state and from that mental state you produce your actions and behaviors.

Sure, there are external triggers that can change our moods in a blink of an eye, but even those triggers can be changed. Those triggers have unconscious meanings that we have given to them at some point of our lives.

In the end, it all comes down to the point that we can affect our health and well-being with our thoughts and choices. In fact, it seems that our thoughts and emotional states have more impact on our health than our genes and DNA!

Many people seem to rely on outside sources, like doctors or a healthcare system, to take care of their health when we have arguably the most effective tool for good health within us: the free choice, based on our own thoughts.

"One of the strongest predictors of health is someone's emotional state."

- Seka Nikolic [1]

"Generally speaking, physical and mental health are attendant upon positive attitudes, whereas ill health, both physical and mental, is associated with such negative attitudes as resentment, jealousy, hostility, self-pity, fear, anxiety, etc."

- Dr. David R. Hawkins [2]

"You can filter your life with rose-colored beliefs that will help your body grow or you can use a dark filter that turns everything black and makes your body/ mind more susceptible to disease. You can live a life of fear or live a life of love. You have the choice! But I can tell you that if you choose to see a world full of love, your body will respond by growing in health. If you choose to believe that you live in a dark world full of fear, your body's health will be compromised as you physiologically close yourself down in a protection response."

- Bruce H. Lipton [3]

"If your immune system has been subject to living in the emotion of stress for too long and has certain genes activated for inflammation and disease, you can turn on new genes for growth and repair and switch off the old genes responsible for disease. And at the same time, these epigenetically altered genes will begin to follow new instructions, making new proteins and programming the body for growth, repair, and healing. This is how you can successfully recondition your body to a new mind."

- Dr. Joe Dispenza [4]

"The news everyone should hear is that gene activity is largely under our control."

- Deepak Chopra and Rudolph E. Tanzi [5]

"In my experience everything we do, say and feel affects our health, so to live a balanced life we need to keep our emotions stable and happy. When our emotions nourish us, our energy is strong, and when our energy is strong, our health is good. By living the life that is meant for us, we heal ourselves at a fundamental level."

- Seka Nikolic [6]

"A negative thought or feeling instantly weakens the body and creates an imbalance of the body's energy flow."

- Dr. David R. Hawkins [7]

"The placebo effect shows that our positive thoughts alone have a huge impact on our well-being. Unfortunately, the same is true for negative memories and thoughts. While positive thoughts lift our spirits and relax our bodies, even involuntary recollections of past grudges, breakups, and arguments lock our minds and bodies into negativity. Repeated experiences of anger and anxiety predispose us to cardiovascular disease, because negative emotions increase the strain on the heart and circulatory system."

- Lauri Nummenmaa [8]

"Your perception of any given thing, at any given moment, can influence the brain chemistry, which, in turn, affects the environment where your cells reside and controls their fate. In other words: your thoughts and perceptions have a direct and overwhelmingly significant effect on cells."

– Dr. Bruce H. Lipton [9]

"It is not surprising that since the way you feel affect your thoughts and attitudes about things, and since your thoughts and attitudes equal your point of attraction, and since your point of attraction equals the way your life continues to play out – *there are a few things of greater value than the achievement of a good-feeling body.*

It is quite interesting to note that not only does a good-feeling body promote positive thoughts, but that, also positive thoughts promote a good-feeling body. That means you do not have to be in a perfect state of health in order to find feelings of relief that eventually can lead to a wonderful mood or attitude, for if you are able to somehow find that relief even when your body is hurting or sick, you will find physical improvement, because your thoughts create your reality."

- Esther and Jerry Hicks [10]

"I absolutely do strongly believe that we *all* have the capacity to heal ourselves as well as facilitate the healing of others. When we get in touch with that infinite place within us where we are Whole, then illness can't remain in the body. And because we're all connected, there's no reason why one person's state of wellness can't touch others, elevating them and triggering their recovery. And when we heal others, we also heal ourselves and the planet. There's no separation except in our own minds."

- Anita Moorjani [11]

"The conclusion is simple: positive perceptions of the mind enhance health by engaging immune functions, while inhibition of immune activities by negative perceptions can participate dis-ease."

- Bruce H. Lipton [12]

"A negative feeling instantly causes a loss of 50% of the body's muscle strength and also narrows our vision both physically and mentally."

- Dr. David R. Hawkins [13]

"While the genes your parents passed on to you won't change into new genes – your unique blueprint stays the same throughout your lifetime – gene activity changes fluidly and very often quickly. Genes are susceptible to adverse change that can occur as the result of diet, disease, stress, and other factors. That's why everyday lifestyle choices have repercussions down to the genetic level."

- Deepak Chopra and Rudolph E. Tanzi [14]

"Healing takes place in the mind as well in the body. Whether someone is suffering from a physical or emotional disease, they always need to look at how they think."

- Seka Nikolic [15]

"For your own health and wellbeing, forgiveness is simply the most energy-efficient option. It frees you from the incredibly toxic, debilitating drain of holding grudge."

-Doc Childre [16]

"Stress, stressful life events and the negative emotions they cause weaken the immune system and make people more susceptible to catching colds, for example. If people are exposed to common pathogens in a laboratory setting, such as noroviruses that cause the flu, stressed and unhappy people get sick significantly more often than non-stressed and happy people. Stress also affects the healing of infectious diseases and the healing of injuries."

- Lauri Nummenmaa [17]

"True wellbeing isn't possible when negativity is undermining it."

- Deepak Chopra and Rudolph E. Tanzi [18]

"Research has shown that a depressed mental state has a direct negative impact on the immune system, not only causing illness but also extending the recovery time. I'm sure I'm not alone in my belief that pessimism attracts poor health and negativity, and that happy and positive feelings attract vitality and robust health."

- Seka Nikolic [19]

"Well-being arises from the fact that actions produce results that align with your own values."

- Lauri Järvilehto [20]

"It appeared that physical illness was really the result of negative belief systems and that the body could actually literally change as a result of the shift of a belief pattern. One is really subject only to what is held in mind."

- Dr. David R. Hawkins [21]

"Stress is one of the biggest causes of epigenetic change, because it knocks your body out of balance."

- Dr. Joe Dispenza [22]

"What you need to understand is that fear causes the greatest damage to our health and is the root of many other negative emotions."

- Seka Nikolic [23]

"It has been shown that maintaining an active, adaptable mind is one of the key factors in staying young."

- Héctor Garcia and Francesc Miralles [24]

"Health, wealth, beauty, and genius are not created; they are only manifested by the arrangement of your mind – that is, by your concept of yourself, and your concept of yourself is all that you accept and consent to as true."

– Neville [25]

"Each of us possesses the ability, at least at some level, to influence our health and control our physical form in ways that are nothing short of dazzling."

-Michael Talbot [26]

"The only way you´re going to have more money, lose weight, be healthier, and feel more fulfilled is if you first change your patterns and ways of thinking."

- Nick Ortner [27]

"Our capacity to understand, forgive, and accept is directly linked to our personal health."

- Dr. David R. Hawkins [28]

Our thoughts create our emotional states, and our emotional states affect our health and well-being. Positive feelings enhance our health and negative emotions weaken it. In a way, it can be said that our body expresses what our mind thinks and believes. Furthermore, we almost invariably make better choices when we are in a positive state of mind.

Do we really need to stress about things? It has been proven that we create better actions and behavior from a more relaxed state (more on that topic in the next chapter).

When we are in a state of stress our thinking narrows down and we are less capable to see more options. Therefore, we tend to repeat the same patterns we have used before. For us to grow and feel better, we need to expand our thinking and try new things.

When you add to that all the negative physiological effects that stress has, wouldn't it be much better to relax a bit and take care of your mind and body?

And to make better choices.

Chapter Seventeen
Actions And Behaviors

How we act and behave in our everyday life largely defines who we become in our lifetime.

Behind every action and behavior there's always a thought – whether a conscious or an unconscious one. Many of those thoughts involve decisions and choices. As we have already learned, we *do* have the freedom to choose our thoughts and, therefore, our actions and behaviors.

How and what we think about creates our actions and behaviors. Most of that process is based on our learned thought patterns and acts on automation. Since they are learned processes, we can always learn new processes, thus producing new types of action and behavior.

We have also established already that every action is based on a target or a goal. The meaning of every action is to achieve something. Let's say the action is scratching your nose. The meaning – and goal – of that action is probably to ease the itching on the nose. This principle applies to all action and behavior, no matter how insignificant or significant.

The point is, when it comes to shaping and experiencing your life in a new way, you need to set new goals, directions, meanings and visions for yourself. That creates new behaviors, which is a part of experiencing life in a new way.

"Living more in harmony with who we truly are isn't just forcing ourselves to repeat positive thoughts. It really means being and doing things that make us happy, things that arouse our passion and bring out the best in us, things that make us feel good—and it also means loving ourselves unconditionally. When we're flowing in this way and feeling upbeat and energized about life, we're in touch with our magnificence. When we can find that within us, things really start getting exciting, and we find synchronicities happening all around us."

- Anita Moorjani [1]

"Every person, all the events of your life are there because you have drawn them there.

What you choose to do with them is up to you."

- Richard Bach [2]

"If there's one thing that life has taught me, it's that it isn't what you're born with or what happens to you in life – it's the choices you make along the way that determines your ultimate destiny."

- Paul McKenna [3]

"You are in charge of your life. You are responsible – no one else – for your choices. No one outside yourself can make you think, do or feel anything you do not choose for yourself."

- Stephen R. Covey [4]

"If you really want to have a more enjoyable life, reaching your goals is not enough. You're also going to have to find a more enjoyable way of getting there."

- Michael Neill [5]

"I think it's important to know where your future is headed, but once you've set yourself on the right path, the only way to get there is by focusing on the here and now. Whatever you do in the next minute, hour and day will play a part in creating your future."

- Seka Nikolic [6]

"For any outcome I want there is a certain way of thinking and acting that will get it for me."

- Bill Harris [7]

"We either make ourselves miserable or we make ourselves strong. The amount of work is the same."

–Carlos Castenada [8]

"What kind of people we are depends on how we think
and behave."
- Lauri Järvilehto [9]

"Don't live down to expectations. Go out there and do
something remarkable."
–Wendy Wasserstein [10]

"Though what you believe does manifest in your life, this
doesn't happen by some sort of magic. What you believe
manifests in your life because you DO something to make
it manifest."
- Bill Harris [11]

"There are ultimately only two big questions in life:

What do I want to do?

How do I get it done?

...Both are key questions of life skills, which together form
the backbone of a good life. And the answer to both
questions is your own life. Even if you have never
consciously thought about these questions, you answer
them every day, with every choice you make."
- Frank Martela [12]

"You have control over only three things in your life—the thoughts you think, the images you visualize, and the actions you take (your behavior)."

- Jack Canfield [13)

"*Plans* are inert and useless without sufficient *power* to translate them into *action*."

- Napoleon Hill [14)

"Action is the foundational key to all success."

—Pablo Picasso [15)

"You don't need to be great to get started, but you need to get started to be great."

—MK Asante [16)

"Hope without action is pointless. Hope with action changes the world."

—Owen Fitzpatrick [17)

"Creating blue oceans is not a static achievement but a dynamic process."

- W. Chan Kim & Renée Mauborgne [18)

"There is only one way to fail: not to try. You can only succeed by trying…Every new endeavor is an experiment in which you explore solutions that work. Finding solutions that don't work also helps you develop yourself."

- Lauri Järvilehto [19]

"You're guaranteed to miss every shot you don't take. So take that shot! Don't brood over one idea or another for two or three years as many people do – give it a go! Don't get lulled into the morass of perpetual paralysis by analysis: if your instinct is positive then go with it. You will learn so many more lessons by just doing than you ever will by mulling it over and over."

- Richard Branson [20]

"The action that fails is way better than no action."

- Bill Harris [21]

"Failure is always a blessing in disguise."

- Napoleon Hill [22]

"It's not so important where we stand but the direction in which we are moving."

-Goethe [23]

"Instead of shaping stupidity, I want you to start to shape your life in a positive direction so that you don't just set goals and achieve them, but you make sure everything that you do makes your whole life better exponentially.

-Richard Bandler [24]

"Action always happens now – not tomorrow or in a week."

- Lauri Järvilehto [25]

"By taking small, seemingly insignificant actions in the direction of our goals and dreams (baby steps), we can quickly create changes which not only lessen the symptoms of depression but can also bring more energy, hope and vitality into our daily lives."

- Michael Neill [26]

"It is not enough to find a purpose that unifies one's goals: one must also carry through and meet its challenges. The purpose must result in strivings; intent has to be translated into action. We may call this *resolution* in the pursuit of one's goals."

- Mihaly Csikszentmihalyi [27]

"Nothing happens until something moves"

-Albert Einstein [28]

"You are growth-seeking Beings, and as you are moving forward, you are at your happiest. When you are having a feeling of stagnation, you are not at your happiest."

- Esther and Jerry Hicks [29]

"Start learning, start focusing your attention, make small steps if that feels more comfortable, but keep on moving, have your end goal in mind all the time. People who make a difference are people who go out in the world, start working on an idea and they learn and improve as they go along."

- Dr. Alexander Sinigoj [30]

"There is no action in all of the Universe that is more delicious than inspired action."

- Esther and Jerry Hicks [31]

"Our behaviour is a function of our decisions, not our conditions."

- Stephen R. Covey [32]

"What I am and what I represent becomes visible through what I do. When a person feels fulfilled – when volunteerism joins hands with expertise – they have found a central source of valuable life. Nothing else is needed.

When I express myself, I am alive and my life is worth living."

— Frank Martela [33]

"Without action there's no possibility of success."

— Richard Bandler and Garner Thomson [34]

"Determine what you want in life and act on it. Stop waiting for someone to give it to you. You'll be waiting a long time."

— Susan Jeffers [35]

"Every day, take at least one action step toward making your goals come true. What you move towards moves toward you."

— Dr. John F. Demartini [36]

"There are so many brilliant people out there who analyze and plan and never get to first base because they don't get out and *do*. The focus is the goal; the action is where the real difference is."

— John Assaraf [37]

"All well-being, whether radical or not, contains two simple steps.

First, find out what's good for you and what's bad.

Second, do what's good for you while avoiding what's bad."
- Deepak Chopra and Rudolph E. Tanzi [38]

"I have discovered that to determine whether my actions stem from "doing" or "being," I only need to look at the emotion behind my everyday decisions. Is it fear, or is it passion? If everything I do each day is driven by passion and a zest for living, then I'm "being," but if my actions are a result of fear, then I'm in "doing" mode.
- Anita Moorjani [39]

"Whatever might have been the cause of a disadvantage in life, the only thing that really matters is what we do about it, and how we live from that moment forward."
- Tina Turner [40]

"Taking action generates happiness. If it feels light, it is the action you need to take."
- Christie Marie Sheldon [41]

"Once you know WHY you do what you do, the question is HOW will you do it? HOWs are your values or principles that guide HOW to bring your cause to life"

- Simon Sinek [42]

"Every time you act, ask yourself, 'Is this aligned with what I think, what I believe and who I want to be?'"

- Roxie Nafousi [43]

"The secret in handling fear is to move yourself from a position of pain to a position of power. The fact that you have the fear then becomes irrelevant."

- Susan Jeffers [44]

"What you believe determines how you act. How you act determines what results you get, and the results you get determine what your beliefs are. It's a cycle: beliefs, actions, results, beliefs."

- Richard Bandler, Alessio Roberti & Owen Fitzpatrick [45]

"Change the belief, and the thinking automatically changes. Change the thinking, and the action changes. Change the action, and the result changes."

- John Assaraf [46]

"Change happens easily when you focus on changing what is within your control – your attitude and your actions."

- Michael Neill [47]

"You create habits by repetition. Each one of our thoughts and actions corresponds to a neural pathway in the brain. The more we repeat a thought or action, the stronger that pathway becomes, just as a footpath across a field becomes more clear and firm the more people walk along it."

- Paul McKenna [48]

"In essence, if we want to direct our lives, we must take control of our consistent action. It's not what we do once in a while that shapes our lives, but what we do consistently."

- Anthony Robbins [49]

"You begin with your thoughts, then thoughts become actions, actions become habits, and habits become part of who you truly are."

- Richard Bandler, Alessio Roberti & Owen Fitzpatrick [50]

"When you get an inspired nudge to take action, then take action. Don't wait. Act. Act right now."

- Joe Vitale [51]

"The function is *what* you get; behaviour is *how* you get it."

- Richard Bandler and John Grinder [52]

"The universe notes and records every action and returns it in kind. Karma is actually the very nature of the universe because of the innate structure and function of the universe itself. In the universe time is measured in eons. Beyond that, it does not even exist at all. Every kindness is therefore forever."

- Dr. David R. Hawkins [53]

"Negative emotions create negative actions and reactions."

- Steven J. Stowell & Matt M. Starcevich [54]

"The simple truth is, we are designed in such a way that our unconscious programming drives our behavior. When our 'rational' thinking mind steps in, it's more often to justify our actions than it is to steer the ship."

- Michael Neill [55]

"When you switch fear to curiosity, you open your eyes and ears and you learn a new behavior."

- Dr. Richard Bandler & Owen Fitzpatrick [56)]

"Your goal should be behavior related, so that it can generate things for you, if your goal is just a 'thing' it may not be sustainable."

–Anders Piper & Alessandro Mora [57)]

"Go out and live your life fearlessly!"

- Anita Moorjani [58)]

"A formula followed by all geniuses, prominent or not, is: Do what you like to do best, and do it to the very best of your ability."

- Dr. David R. Hawkins [59)]

To recap, actions and behaviors represent your thoughts and choices. They also largely determine what results you achieve in your life, what kind of life you will have, and what kind of circumstances you will live in.

Being clear with your meaning and purpose and knowing what your highest values are, you build a foundation for your goals and directions. When you then start to take action based on that foundation, making sure that you love what you are doing, you are creating a more meaningful life for yourself.

If, on the other hand, you find yourself doing a lot of things in your life that don't feel good to you, that should be a signal for you that you are moving in the wrong direction.

Chapter Eighteen

Thought

It all begins with a thought.

Our thoughts guide all our feelings, actions and behaviors. By far, most of our thoughts act as unconscious programs that are running in the background. They are mainly based on our beliefs, habits, paradigms and values.

The thing is, we *can choose* our thoughts once we become aware of them. In fact, our thoughts are pretty much the only thing we have a *full control* of in our lives.

Some thought patterns are harder to change, some are easier. But your thoughts are *your* thoughts, and *you* create them in your mind. Therefore, *you* are the one who can change them!

To change your thinking, awareness is the key. As long as the thoughts are running as automations in the background, it is practically impossible to chance them. Once you become aware of your thoughts, however, you have the possibility to do something about them.

And once you change your thinking, everything that follows changes.

"Moments are the currency of life. The quality of your thoughts equals the quality of your life."

- Kalliope Barlis [1]

"Maybe reality isn't what you think it is. Maybe whatever you think becomes your reality."
   - Richard Bandler, Alessio Roberti & Owen Fitzpatrick [2]

"As we transform our thoughts, we transform our feelings and transform our lives."
   -Blanca Diez [3]

"If how you think and how you feel broadcasts an electromagnetic signature that influences every area of your life, you are broadcasting the same electromagnetic energy and your life never changes."
   - Dr. Joe Dispenza [4]

"The process of taking charge of your life and changing the way you think, feel and behave starts at the attitude level."
   - Owen Fitzpatrick [5]

"We're living in the feeling of our thinking, not the feeling of the world."
   - Michael Neill [6]

"Marcus Aurelius, the great Roman philosopher and sage, said, "A man's life is what his thoughts make of it." The leading American philosopher of the nineteenth century, Ralph Waldo Emerson, said, "A man is what he thinks all day long." The thoughts you habitually entertain in your mind have the tendency to actualize themselves in physical conditions."

- Joseph Murphy [7)]

"What are Mind, Consciousness, and Thought?

Mind is the intelligence of all things; Consciousness makes you aware; and Thought is like the rudder of a ship. It guides you through life, and if you learn to use that rudder properly, you can guide your way through life far better than you ever imagined."

-Syd Banks [8)]

We can take charge of our thoughts. But if the vast majority of them are running as automations in the background, how can we become aware of them and thus change them?

Our thoughts create our feelings and actions. Therefore, it is extremely useful to pay attention to your emotional state: if you are in a negative emotional state, what are you doing at that moment and where is the focus of your thoughts?

I can predict with certainty that at that moment your focus is on something you would like to avoid in your life and your actions are not taking you toward the life you want.

If, on the other hand, you are feeling good and joyful, it is certain that the focus of your thoughts is on something that you'd like more in your life and the chances are that you are doing something that moves you toward the life you want.

The latter isn't, however, always so. It is possible that even when you are in a positive emotional state, you might not be moving toward the life you want. It is possible that you are somehow misguided. There are other pleasures in life that are not taking you where you want to go in the long term. Unfortunately, many of those pleasures are addictive and destructive.

Therefore, it is essential to remind yourself from time to time of what your purpose in life is, what are your highest values and what is the vision of life you want to create, and evaluate again what you are doing and where the focus of your thoughts is.

Whenever you are in a negative emotional state, pay attention to what you are thinking at that moment. You will realize that your thoughts are on something that you would like to avoid in your life. By stopping and paying attention to your feelings is a good way to become aware of your thoughts. And like said, once you are aware of your thoughts you can change them if you want to.

When you keep your thoughts on your purpose and act accordingly, you should feel good about your actions. As a byproduct, you are creating the life you want ☺.

Chapter Nineteen
Miscellaneous Wisdoms

To this last chapter, I have collected some wise words that do not quite fit in the topics of the chapters above or they might contain wisdoms that might fit in more than one of the chapters. Some of these quotes are also more general in nature, however not any less significant.

I am sure you can give them your own categories in your mind and take the wisdom they offer.

"The proper function of a man is to live, not to exist."

-Jack London [1]

"How you feel in any one moment is more important than anything else, because how you feel right now is creating your life."

- Rhonda Byrne [2]

"The quality of your life is not the quality of your events, it is the meaning you attached to your events."

–Anthony Robbins [3]

"Optimists have not become optimists because they have always had good luck. Instead, optimists have generally always succeeded precisely because they are optimists. Optimism is faith in the future: the belief that things will work out. But how things work out depends significantly on how you act yourself."

- Lauri Järvilehto [4]

"But that's life, a kind of coin toss. Sometimes you get heads and sometimes you get tails. You have to adapt to that, but the game goes on until the final whistle."

- Jari Litmanen [5]

"In your life you find what you seek: if you focus on problems, you'll find problems wherever you go; if you look for solutions, you'll find solutions."

- Richard Bandler, Alessio Roberti & Owen Fitzpatrick [6]

"We are not victims of our genes, but masters of our fates, able to create lives overflowing with peace, happiness, and love."

- Bruce H. Lipton [7]

"The amount you suffer in life is directly related to how much you are resisting the fact that things are the way they are."

- Bill Harris [8]

"Without enjoyment life can be endured, and it can even be pleasant. But it can be so only precariously, depending on luck and the cooperation of the external environment. To gain personal control over the quality of experience, however, one needs to learn how to build enjoyment into what happens day in, day out."

- Mihaly Csikszentmihalyi [9]

"If there is a meaning in life at all, then there must be a meaning in suffering. Suffering is an ineradicable part of life, even as fate and death. Without suffering and death human life cannot be complete."

- Viktor E. Frankl [10]

"Every problem in this life is temporary, while solutions can offer permanent change to live your life's purpose."

- Kalliope Barlis [11]

"In life, you will have good things happen and bad things happen. You can't always control what happens, but you can always control how you deal with it."
   - Richard Bandler, Alessio Roberti & Owen Fitzpatrick [12)]

"It's in your moments of decision that your destiny is shaped."

- Anthony Robbins [13)]

"In the Kalama Sutta the Buddha says, don't believe what I say, don't believe what is "logical" or handed down to you by tradition. But whatever is beneficial to you and to others, that is praised by the wise – take it and use it. And what is harmful to you, obstructive, and makes difficulty, well, then leave it aside. So you are the arbiter of what is true and good by your own experience and you learn your own lessons."

– Ajahn Amaro [14)]

"*Associate with pleasant memories*, and *dissociate from unpleasant ones.*"

- Richard Bandler [15)]

"When a young man asked Carlyle how he should go about reforming the world, Carlyle answered, 'Reform yourself.

That way there will be one less rascal in the world.' The advice is still valid. Those who try to make life better for everyone without having learned to control their own lives first usually end up making things worse all around."

- Mihaly Csikszentmihalyi [16)]

"Here are the three main steps to caring for yourself as an empath:

1. Undo. You have to *undo* so you can *be*. When we're trying to change an aspect of our lives, our inclination is to start doing—buying books, signing up for classes, doing five things that scare us each day—but first, we have to make space. Instead, we can work toward releasing and letting go of what no longer serves us. If we can take the time to pause and sit with ourselves, we can make space for the solutions to come to us, rather than going out and searching for them...
2. Love yourself as though your life depends on it, because, believe me, it does. For each and every item you say yes to, ask yourself, Does this event/thought/person make me feel lighter, or does it weigh me down?
3. Deepen your intuition. After you undo, your essence is pure. You can open the space for self-love, and your intuition will naturally open."

- Anita Moorjani [17)]

"The less we have on our mind, the better life gets."

- Michael Neill [18]

"I believe that happiness is best found as a byproduct of a meaningful life. A life where you focus on self-realization and doing good for other people."

- Frank Martela [19]

Chapter Twenty

Conclusion

There are several different concepts and theories about levels of consciousness and personal growth.

Consciousness is a multidimensional and complex concept that can be interpreted in many different ways. At its simplest, it refers to a person being aware of themselves and the world around them. This means the ability to perceive, experience, feel, and understand things.

The experience of consciousness is therefore a complex process involving brain function, mental state, and social interaction. It is also connected to our identity, personality, and how we experience the world and reality around us.

Consciousness is also an important concept in philosophy, psychology, neuroscience, and spiritual traditions. It involves many profound questions about the nature, origin, and meaning of consciousness, which have inspired extensive research and reflection throughout human history.

Furthermore, consciousness is associated with our experience of reality. People experience reality through their own consciousness and perceptions. Traditionally, reality is understood as the physical world we live in, and which is observable through our senses. However, philosophers, psychologists and scientists have long debated how our minds process, interpret and construct reality.

Vibrational Frequencies of Consciousness

Our thoughts and feelings are made up of energy. This can be verified with modern technologies like the EEG, fMRI and CT scans. Also, different emotions have different frequencies. This you can easily feel in your body.

When we change our thoughts, we change how we feel and what emotions we experience, which in turn changes our entire vibrational frequency. Therefore, when we change our thoughts and thus our emotions, we can change our vibration and ultimately our reality.

There are various tables of our vibrational frequencies, and they differ somewhat. Below I will present the scale of consciousness presented by Dr. David R. Hawkins, which is based on extensive research and mapping conducted since the 1980s.

Level		Frequency	Emotion	Process
Enlightenment	⇑	700-1000	Ineffable	Pure Consciousness
Peace	⇑	600	Bliss	Illumination
Joy	⇑	540	Serenity	Transformation
Love	⇑	500	Reverence	Revelation
Reason	⇑	400	Understanding	Abstraction
Acceptance	⇑	350	Forgiveness	Trancendence
Willigness	⇑	310	Optimism	Intention
Neutrality	⇑	250	Trust	Release
Courage	⇕	200	Affirmation	Empowerment
Pride	⇓	175	Scorn	Inflation
Anger	⇓	150	Hate	Aggression
Desire	⇓	125	Craving	Enslavement
Fear	⇓	100	Anxiety	Withdrawal
Grief	⇓	75	Regret	Despondency
Apathy	⇓	50	Despair	Abdication
Guilt	⇓	30	Blame	Destruction
Shame	⇓	20	Humiliation	Elimination

Abridged table from Dr. David R. Hawkins' table [1]

In the table, the frequency of 200, courage, is the frequency where negativity changes to positive and vice versa. Below 200, negative vibration is produced by levels and emotional states such as pride, anger, greed, fear, sadness, despair and shame. Similarly, above 200, there are such states as trust, optimism, forgiveness, understanding, love, joy and peace.

According to Dr. Hawkins, humanity is heavily programmed at negative levels of consciousness, meaning that 78 percent of the world's population is below level 200, the level of courage and empowerment. In addition, his research shows that only four percent of the world's population reaches level 500 of love, and only 0.4 percent reaches level 540, which is joy and unconditional love.

Approximately one in ten million people (0.000001 percent) reaches the level of enlightenment at level 700 of consciousness.

The Concept of The Four Levels of Consciousness

Another way to understand the levels of consciousness is the theory of the four stages of consciousness and spiritual growth, which I believe was developed by Dr. Michael Beckwith [2].

The four stages of consciousness and spiritual growth concept – or theory, whatever you like – is based on the idea that at any given moment we view the world based on our emotional state, which is filtered through the quality of our own consciousness. We can experience our reality through, among other things, life events, beliefs, patterns, programming, and various learned traits. Or it can be experienced based on what we first view of ourselves.

The process presented by Dr. Beckwith is continuous and often lifelong. The goal is that we move through each stage as we grow spiritually.

In my experience, we can be in all four stages, even during the same day, but only at different times. However, there is one level where we spend most of our time. Unfortunately, it also seems that most people live constantly on the two lowest levels.

In the following, I will briefly present Dr. Beckwith's four stages of consciousness and spiritual growth – or at least my own interpretations of them. As you can see, it also follows to some extent Dr. David R. Hawkins' view of the different levels.

Stage 1: To Me – Victim Stage

At this level, a person feels that life is happening to them. Our problems are outside of ourselves, in our environment. We are victims of our circumstances and much of our time is spent whining and complaining, like, "Why does this always happen to me?"

You move to the second stage when you realize that you are not a victim and that the world does not happen to you, but for you.

Stage 2: By Me – Awakening

At this level, we feel that we have some control over what happens to us. We understand that change is possible, we can set goals and intentions. We start to use the power of our mind, begin to study self-development, we challenge things and our environment, we begin to change things around us. We start to manifest things into our lives by creative visualizations.

Stage 3: Through Me – Recoding

At this level, we discover that our inner world has its own reality. We begin to develop and practice qualities and skills such as forgiveness, compassion, letting go, gratitude, and manifestation. We begin to shape and recode ourselves, and through that, we also change the world around us. We spend more and more time in a state of flow, allowing things happen through us, surrendering to the universe and universal laws.

Stage 4: As Me – Connection

At this highest level, we experience a connection and understanding of belonging to something greater than ourselves. We feel deep compassion for all living things and can see the world without judgment or attachment to people, things, or outcomes. The highest level of this stage is called enlightenment where we feel we are one with the universe.

Logical Levels

The Logical Levels model is based on Gregory Bateson's teachings of Ecology of Mind. Bateson's works has then been modified by several people, including Dr. Richard Bandler and his student Robert Dilts.

There are also different variations of the model. For example, Dilts puts values and beliefs together to the same level, whereas some other people, like Kathleen La Valle, puts values higher than beliefs. On the other hand, Bandler does not regard the levels of purpose or identity like Dilts does.

The version I present below is a combination of all the above.

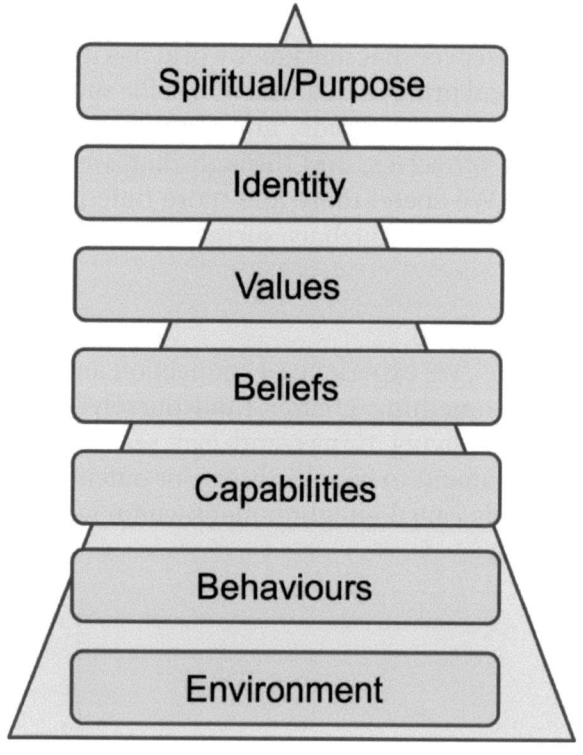

The Logical Levels model refers to a hierarchy of levels of processes within an individual or a group. The function in each level is to synthesize, organize and direct the interactions on the levels below it. Something on an upper level is supposed to 'radiate' downward, facilitating change on the lower levels. Something on a low-level could, but would not necessarily, affect the upper levels.

The model provides a framework for deciding at what level to work to bring about the required change. In other words, the model takes a systemic approach to change rather than a one-dimensional approach.

The Process of Personal Growth

As we study all three models/concepts presented above we easily come to realize that there are some fundamental similarities in them.

They are all based on the observation that on the lowest level we work on and are affected by the environment. For example, in Hawkins' model basically everything below the scale of 150 is caused by a person reacting to the environment, and that is also what the Logical Levels and the Four Stages consider to be the lowest level.

All three concepts also consider some form of spirituality to be the highest level of human development.

Furthermore, we can see that somewhere between the highest and the lowest levels are things that are related to our beliefs and values.

The reason why I'm saying all this is that I think it is safe to say that several studies suggest that there is an observable pattern in our personal growth, and it starts from being a victim of circumstances or environment and ends up with high spiritual experiences, even enlightenment.

For most of us, personal growth is a gradual process where we move from the lower stages toward the higher ones. Very few of us, it seems, can take a giant leap and have a transformational experience that will change the way they think and experience their lives. This is not, however, totally unusual.

Personal growth, whether gradual or fast, is based on a change in thinking. When you think in a different way, you experience life in a different way. Changing the way we think, however, is usually difficult because our brain likes what is familiar to it and once we have made up our mind about something, it is most of the times hard for us to admit that we were wrong. This applies especially when we are still in the lower levels in our development.

How does one change their thinking, then? How do we reprogram ourselves in a way that enables growth and ascend in the stages of consciousness?

For the lower levels, there are a lot of different techniques and methods, of which I have found neuro-linguistic programming (NLP) and hypnosis to be probably the most effective. Other methods include EFT (Emotional Freedom Technique), Wingwave (which uses also NLP), Havening, and different kinds of coaching, to name but a few.

My previous books *Better Life and NLP* and particularly *Your Own Blue Ocean* are focused especially on advice and techniques that are designed to help you rise from the lower levels (200 and below on Dr. Hawkins' scale of consciousness and stages 1-2 on Dr. Beckwith's four levels of consciousness) to the levels of higher awareness and consciousness.

In my experience the more you grow and advance in the levels of consciousness, the less there are techniques and methods to aid you. Perhaps the only one I know is meditation. However, there are many different ways to meditate and one that is of best use for someone might not be what helps you the most.

As you approach the frequency level of 400 on Dr. Hawkins' scale of consciousness and advance further, it is my understanding and experience that the growth becomes more and more an internal process of awareness, reflection, intuition and inspiration.

When you read and listen to the teachings of enlightened people, they tell you that the experience becomes less and less describable in words. It becomes a process you can only experience. The moment you try to put the experience in words, you will necessarily have to generalize, distort and delete information because our language in incapable to describe the experience as it really is.

I have selected quotes with my comments and interpretations to this book that cover more or less all the stages of personal growth, all the way from external stimuli to inner peace and spiritual awakening. I have, however, excluded quotes that directly address enlightenment. Despite its nobility and Divinity, enlightenment is beyond the scope of this book.

My hope is that many of the quotes and/or my comments have evoked insights and inspirations in you and that they will give further guidance in your journey of personal growth. All quotes in this book certainly have inspired me in many ways!

The Ultimate Ambition of This Book

I believe that when people behave and make decisions from states like joy, love and acceptance, instead of states like anger, fear or blame, they make better decisions and they behave more constructively, not destructively.

I further believe that when more and more people in the world behave and make decisions from the frequency above 200 in Dr. Hawkins' scale of consciousness, we make the world a better place collectively.

I hope this book has given you insights and moments of inspiration for your own journey on the path of personal growth. I further hope that you have gained some more awareness on how you can improve your own life and rise higher on the scale of consciousness.

Ultimately, I hope you continue growing and that you will join the increasing number of people who live more and more in positive states, who make better decisions and who behave in ways that will benefit not only you but also this planet that we all share.

Appendixes

Acknowledgments

There are so many people who have helped me with my growth. I have learned from an immense number of people an enormous amount of skills and knowledge that it is impossible to mention and thank each and every one of them here.

It also impossible for me to rank them for what they have given me. Some of the knowledge learned from someone might have been exactly what I needed at that point of my life, some knowledge I have gained from some people during a long period of time.

There are some who have helped immensely with just one of their books I've read or a course or seminar I've attended. Sometimes just one thought or a sentence has been all I needed to move forward with my growth.

The End Notes and Bibliography, that will follow, list most of those people whose advice I highly appreciate. I recommend that you familiarize yourself with the list carefully and choose what is suitable for you to read.

That is why I am listing below only a few of the most significant people that I have had a long-lasting personal contact with, and who have had a strong influence on me, in one way or another (in alphabetical order).

Individuals

Dr. Richard Bandler: Richard is the genius behind neuro-linguistic programming (NLP) and I have had the privilege to attend dozens of his seminars, first as a student and later as a member of the international team of assistant trainers. I have also read probably about 97 % of the dozens of books he has authored. In short, with the help of the techniques and tools of NLP, I was able to get myself out of the lower levels of consciousness and personal growth and gained an understanding of human mind that has been of indispensable on my path.

Chris Cummins: Chris is a fellow Master Trainer of NLP and the Co-Owner and Joint Managing Director of Our Training Department (OTD), based in Birmingham, England. Chris has been a big inspiration and role model for me. His positivity, skills and helpfulness has guided me on several occasions.

Bill Harris: Bill was involved in personal development for nearly 40 years as a seeker, teacher, public speaker, author, therapist and workshop leader. He studied and practiced a wide range of traditional and modern transformational and therapeutic practices. His great legacy lives on in his life-changing online courses, best-selling books and Holosync® neuro-audio technology. I attended Bill's year-long coaching program and attended several of his courses. Bill taught me a lot about meditation and NLP.

Juha Kivinen: Juha is a Mental Coach and a Shaman. He and I met over 15 years ago in an NLP course and attended several courses, trainings and seminars together as years went by. For the last ten years or so, Juha and I have held weekly skype calls, where we spar and help each other as coaches and entrepreneurs. He also helped me remarkably with my fourth book (which has not yet been translated to English).

John and Kathleen La Valle: John and Kathleen run the Society of NLP™ and Richard Bandler's seminars. They both also teach together with Richard and have taught me a lot of NLP. Thanks to John and Kathleen, I also had the chance to become a member of the international team of assistant trainers in Richard's seminars, an experience that has been priceless for me.

Anders Piper: Anders is a Master Trainer of NLP and Psychologist. I have attended several of Anders' advanced NLP courses and learned a lot from him. He was one of my most important teachers in the early years of my career.

Bob Proctor: Bob was a new thought self-help author and business owner. He was best known for his best-selling book *You Were Born Rich* and being a contributor to the film *The Secret*. I attended Bob's year-long coaching program and invited him to hold a seminar in Helsinki, Finland. During the seminar in Helsinki in 2011, I had some valuable conversations with him that provided me with great help at that time on my journey.

Timo Räkköläinen: Timo is the Founder and Head Teacher of HIPKO (Helsinki Self-Defense School). He first stepped into my life as my master in martial arts approximately 25 years ago. In addition to the finesse of martial arts, he also gave me my first contacts with the world of meditation. Through the years he has become a dear friend to me and a godfather to my son. We have shared many insightful and illuminating conversations and he has helped with all of my books with his feedback and suggestions. We also went to several NLP courses together some 15 years ago.

Tina Taylor: Tina is a Master Trainer of NLP and a teacher of clinical hypnotherapy. Tina was the Head Teacher in the International College of Clinical Hypnotherapy (ICCH) in London where I studied and got my Diploma in Clinical Hypnotherapy. She also cohosted an enlightening Business Alchemy Retreat in Glastonbury, England with Steve Grabb. In addition, Tina provided me tremendous help with the translation of my book *Your Own Blue Ocean*.

Carolyn Wade: Carolyn is a Self-Care Coach, based in London, England. She was the one who first introduced me to personal development over 30 years ago. Throughout the years we have kept in touch and shared our knowledge of human potential and growth with each other.

Kristine Wollweber: My partner and love for two and half years now. Kristine shares my passion to help people with their problems and although we share the same background of NLP and hypnotherapy, we also have our unique skills and techniques of whose effectiveness we instructively debate every now and then.

Groups of People

My Coaching Clients and Students: Without my clients and students I wouldn't be who I am today. From each client I learn more about coaching: what works and what doesn't. Every client is unique and every coaching session with them is a growth experience for me, too. The same goes to my NLP students. Every student comes to my courses with their own agenda, their own issues and ambitions. Being able to teach them skills that will help them for the rest of their lives is a blessing and seeing the transformations in them during my courses is what keeps me going and growing.

My Fellow Team Members in the International Team of Assistant Trainers at Richard Bandler's Seminars: It is always a joy and privilege to be with them in seminars, whether in the US or in Europe. I thoroughly enjoy sharing skills, drills and knowledge with these guys. I feel there is so much we always learn from each other!

End Notes

Chapter One

1) Esther and Jerry Hicks: Ask and It Is Given, p. 7, Hay House, 2004, 2005, 2008

2) Mihaly Csikszentmihalyi: Flow, The Classic Work on How to Achieve Happiness, p. 6, Rider, 2002

3) Bill Harris: Thresholds of the Mind, page 119, Centerpointe Press, 2007

4) Susan Jeffers: Feel The Fear and Do It Anyway, p. 55, Vermilion, 1987, 2007, 2012

5) Richard Bandler and Owen Fitzpatrick: Patterns for Problem Solving, p. 30, NLP Tranceformations inc., 2022

6) Alan Watts: The Essential Alan Watts, p. 65, Transformational Book Circle, 2006

7) Paul McKenna: Change Your Life in Seven Days, page 88, Bantam Press, 2004

8) Derren Brown: Tricks of the Mind, p. 174, Transworld Publishers, 2007

9) Sandra Ingerman & Hank Wesselman: Awakening to the Spirit World, p. 113, Sounds True, 2010

10) Richard Bach: Illusions, p. 113, Arrow Books, 1977

11) Robert Anton Wilson: Prometheus Rising, p. 1, Hilaritas Press, 1983

12) Jamie Smart: The Little Book of Clarity, p. 183, Capstone, 2015

13) Tina Turner: Happiness Becomes You, p. 70, Astra Books, 2020

14) Michael Neill: Super Coach, p. 24, Hay House

15) Michael Neill: The Inside Out Revolution, page 23, Hay House

16) Susan Jeffers: Feel The Fear and Do It Anyway, p. 56, Vermilion, 1987, 2007, 2012

17) Esther and Jerry Hicks: Money and the Law of Attraction, p. 208, Hay House, 2008

Chapter Two

1) David Perlmutter and Alberto Villoldo: Power Up Your Brain, p. 164, Hay House, 2011
2) Dr. Joe Dispenza: Becoming Supernatural, p. 280-281, Hay House, Inc., 2017, 2019
3) Richard Bandler & John La Valle: Persuasion Engineering™, page 136, Meta Publications Inc., 1996
4) Simon Sinek: Start with Why, p. 11, Penguin Business, 2009
5) David R. Hawkins: The Eye of the I, p. 233, Hay House, 2001
6) Carlos Castaneda: The Fire from Within, p.37, Touchstone Books, 1998
7) Richard Bandler, Alessio Roberti & Owen Fitzpatrick: How to Take Charge of Your Life, page 49, HarperCollinsPublishers, 2014
8) Robert Anton Wilson: Quantum Psychology, page 40, New Falcon Publications, 1990
9) David R. Hawkins: Power vs. Force, p. 291 Hay House, 1995, 1998, 2004, 2012
10) Stephen R. Covey: The 7 Habits of Highly Effective People, p. 36, Simon & Schuster, 1989, 2004
11) Richard Bandler and Owen Fitzpatrick: Patterns for Problem Solving, p. 53, NLP Tranceformations inc.
12) Paul McKenna: Change Your Life in Seven Days, page 12, Bantam Press, 2004
13) David R. Hawkins: The Eye of the I, p. 252, Hay House, 2001
14) Joe Vitale: The Attractor Factor, page 145, John Wiley & Sons, Inc.
15) Tina Turner: Happiness Becomes You, p. 77, Astra Books, 2020
16) Paul McKenna: The 3 Things That Will Change Your Destiny Today, p. 62, Bantam Press, 2015
17) Seka Nikolic: You Can Heal Yourself, p. 208, Pan Books, 2007

18) David R. Hawkins: Transcending The Levels of Consciousness, p. 143, Hay House, 2006

19) Richard Bandler & Owen Fitzpatrick: Conversations with Richard Bandler, page 286, Health Communications, Inc., 2009

Chapter Three

1) Robert Anton Wilson: Prometheus Rising, p. 197, Hilaritas Press, 1983

2) Napoleon Hill: The Master-Key to Riches, p.473, Penguin Books Ltd./JMW Group Inc., 1945, 2007

3) Bill Harris: Thresholds of the Mind, page 119-120, Centerpointe Press

4) Richard Bandler, Alessio Roberti & Owen Fitzpatrick: How to Take Charge of Your Life, page 15, HarperCollins*Publishers*, 2014

5) Bruce H. Lipton: The Biology of Belief, p. 138, Hay House, 2015

6) David R. Hawkins: Transcending The Levels of Consciousness, p. 183, Hay House, 2006

7) Dr. Joe Dispenza: You Are the Placebo, p. 96, Hay House Inc., 2014

Chapter Four

1) Richard Bandler, Alessio Roberti and Owen Fitzpatrick: The Ultimate Introduction to NLP, page 121, HarperCollins *Publishers*, 2013

2) Rob Kosberg: Publish. Promote. Profit™., p. 5, 2018

3) Paul McKenna: Change Your Life in Seven Days, page 20, Bantam Press, 2004

4) John Assaraf: Having it All, p. 136, Atria Books, 2007

5) Dean Graziosi: Millionaire Success habits, p. 66-67, Growth Publishing, 2017

6) Brendon Burchard: The Motivation Manifesto, page 30, Hay House, Inc, 2014

7) Richard Bandler, Alessio Roberti & Owen Fitzpatrick: How to Take Charge of Your Life, page 2, HarperCollins*Publishers*, 2014

8) Frank Martela: Valonöörit, p. 82, Gummerrus Kustannus Oy, 2015

Chapter Five

1) Richard Bandler: Get the Life You Want, p. 175, Harper*Element* 2008
2) Anthony Robbins: Awaken the Giant Within, p. 274, Free Press, 2003
3) Paul McKenna: Change Your Life in Seven Days, page 100, Bantam Press, 2004
4) Frank Martela: Valonöörit, p. 163, Gummerrus Kustannus Oy, 2015
5) Richard Bandler, Alessio Roberti & Owen Fitzpatrick: How to Take Charge of Your Life, page 84-85, HarperCollins*Publishers*, 2014
6) Esther and Jerry Hicks: Ask and It Is Given, p. 27, Hay House, 2004, 2005, 2008
7) Dean Graziosi: Millionaire Success habits, p. 28, Growth Publishing, 2017
8) Bobbe Sommer and Maxwell Maltz: Psycho-cybernetics 2000, page 151, Prentice Hall Press, 2000
9) Paul McKenna: Change Your Life in Seven Days, page 123, Bantam Press, 2004
10) Mihaly Csikszentmihalyi: Flow, The Classic Work on How to Achieve Happiness, p. 216, Rider, 2002
11) Bobbe Sommer and Maxwell Maltz: Psycho-cybernetics 2000, page 12, Prentice Hall Press, 2000
12) David R. Hawkins: Transcending The Levels of Consciousness, p. 95, Hay House, 2006

Chapter Six

1) Anik Singal: The Circle of Profit, p. 55, Lurn Inc., 2016
2) Jari Sarasvuo: Sisäinen sankari, s. 280, WSOY 1996.
3) Tim Ferriss: Tools of Titans, p. 373, Houghton Mifflin Harcourt, 2017
4) Frank Martela: Valonöörit, p. 89, Gummerrus Kustannus Oy, 2015
5) Richard Branson: The Virgin Way, p. 241, Virgin Books, 2015

6) Paul McKenna: Change Your Life in Seven Days, page 122, Bantam Press, 2004

7) Viktor E. Frankl: Man's Search for Meaning, p. 67, Beacon Press, 2006

8) Mihaly Csikszentmihalyi: Flow, The Classic Work on How to Achieve Happiness, p. 217, Rider, 2002

9) Esther and Jerry Hicks: Ask and It Is Given, p. 103, Hay House, 2004, 2005, 2008

10) Frank Martela: Valonöörit, p. 256, Gummerrus Kustannus Oy, 2015

11) Kalliope Barlis: Phobia Relief, p. 25, Building Your Best Publications, 2016

12) Anita Moorjani: Dying to Be Me, p. 159, Hay House, 2012, 2022

13) Richard Bach: Illusions, p. 121, Arrow Books, 1977

14) Richard Bandler & John La Valle: Persuasion Engineering™, page 93, Meta Publications Inc., 1996

Chapter Seven

1) Dan S. Bagley III and Edward J. Reese: Beyond Selling, p. 13, Meta Publications, 1988

2) Kalliope Barlis: Phobia Relief, p. 22, Building Your Best Publications, 2016

3) Robert Dilts, Tim Hallbom and Suzi Smith: Beliefs, page 115, Crown House Publishing Ltd, 2012

4) Stephen R. Covey: The 7 Habits of Highly Effective People, p. 105, Simon & Schuster, 1989, 2004

5) David R. Hawkins: The Eye of the I, p. 287, Hay House, 2001

6) Richard Bandler, Alessio Roberti & Owen Fitzpatrick: How to Take Charge of Your Life, page 118, HarperCollins*Publishers*, 2014

7) Frank Martela: Valonöörit, p. 164, Gummerrus Kustannus Oy, 2015

8) Lauri Järvilehto: Tee itsestäsi mestariajattelija, page 188, Kustannusosakeyhtiö Tammi, 2012

9) David R. Hawkins: Letting Go, p. 150, Hay House, 2018

10) Dr. David R. Hawkins: The Eye of the I, p. 299, Hay House, 2001

11) Michael D. Yapko: Essentials of Hypnosis, p. 22, Routledge, 2015

12) Bruce H. Lipton: The Biology of Belief, p. 138, Hay House, 2015

13) Esther and Jerry Hicks: Ask and It Is Given, p. 184, Hay House, 2004, 2005, 2008

14) Bill Harris: Life Principles Integration Process, Course 2, Lesson 10, Paragraph 71

15) Dr. Joe Dispenza: You Are the Placebo, p. 166, Hay House Inc., 2014

16) John Assaraf: Having it All, page 97, Atria Books

17) Dr. Wayne W. Dyer: Wishes Fulfilled, p. 27-28, Hay House, inc. 2012

18) Bruce H. Lipton: The Biology of Belief, p. 229, Hay House, 2015

19) Joe Vitale: Zero Limits, p. 160, John Wiley & Sons Inc. 2007

20) Richard Bandler, John La Valle, Anders Piper, Alessio Roberti, Alessandro Mora, Kate Benson, Garner Thomson, Owen Fitzpatrick: Seven Practical Applications of NLP, p. 88, Attrakt BV, 2012

21) Derren Brown: Tricks of the Mind, p. 277, Transworld Publishers, 2007

22) Robert Dilts: Changing Belief Systems with NLP, p. 9, Meta Publications, 1990

23) Paul McKenna: Instant Influence & Charisma, p. 149, Bantam Press, 2015

24) Richard Bandler, Alessio Roberti & Owen Fitzpatrick: How to Take Charge of Your Life, page 71, HarperCollins*Publishers*, 2014

25) Michael S. Gazzaniga: Who's in Charge?, p. 2, Robinson, 2016

26) Owen Fitzpatrick: Conversations with Richard Bandler, page 50, Health Communications, Inc.

27) Bruce H. Lipton: The Biology of Belief, p. xxvi, Hay House, 2015

28) Dr. Richard Bandler & Owen Fitzpatrick: Thinking on Purpose, p. 19, New Thinking Publications, 2019

29) Robert Anton Wilson: Cosmic Trigger II – Down to Earth, p. 58, New Falcon Publications, 1995

30) Richard Bandler, John La Valle, Anders Piper, Alessio Roberti, Alessandro Mora, Kate Benson, Garner Thomson, Owen Fitzpatrick: Seven Practical Applications of NLP, p. 88, Attrakt BV, 2012

31) Dr. John F. Demartini: The Breakthrough Experience™, p. 14, Hay House, 2002

32) Jillian Michaels: Unlimited, page 83, Three Rivers Press

Chapter Eight

1) Paul McKenna: Instant Influence & Charisma, p. 149, Bantam Press, 2015

2) Sandra Ingerman & Hank Wesselman: Awakening to the Spirit World, p. 102, Sounds True, 2010

3) Jillian Michaels: Unlimited, page 83, Three Rivers Press

4) Dr Richard Bandler & Owen Fitzpatrick: Memories. Hope is the Question, p. 143, Mysterious Publications, 2014

5) Robert Anton Wilson: Cosmic Trigger II – Down to Earth, p. 70, New Falcon Publications, 1995

6) David R. Hawkins: The Eye of the I, p. 253, Hay House, 2001

7) Dr. Wayne W. Dyer: Wishes Fulfilled, p. 93, Hay House, inc. 2012

8) Dr Richard Bandler & Owen Fitzpatrick: Memories. Hope is the Question, p. 87, Mysterious Publications, 2014

9) Richard Bandler, Alessio Roberti & Owen Fitzpatrick: How to Take Charge of Your Life, page 1, HarperCollins*Publishers*, 2014

10) Bruce H. Lipton: The Biology of Belief, p. 147, Hay House, 2015

11) Jack Canfield, Mark Victor Hansen & Amy Newmark: Chicken Soup for the Soul (20th Anniversary Edition), p. 198, Chicken Soup for the Soul Publishing, 2013

12) Napoleon Hill: The Master-Key to Riches, p.358, Penguin Books Ltd./JMW Group Inc., 1945, 2007

13) David R. Hawkins: The Eye of the I, p. 151, Hay House, 2001

14) Richard Bandler: Guide to Transformation, page xviii, Health Communications, Inc., 2008

15) Dr. John F. Demartini: The Breakthrough Experience™, p. 151, Hay House, 2002
16) Bruce H. Lipton: The Biology of Belief, p. 158, Hay House, 2015
17) Ulla Suokko: Signs of the Universe, p.125, WiseWoman, 2020
18) Mihaly Csikszentmihalyi: Flow, p. 115, Rider, 2002
19) Richard Bandler, Alessio Roberti & Owen Fitzpatrick: How to Take Charge of Your Life, page 12, HarperCollins*Publishers*, 2014
20) Jillian Michaels: Unlimited, page 94, Three Rivers Press
21) Susan Jeffers: Feel The Fear and Do It Anyway, p. 192, Vermilion, 1987, 2007, 2012
22) David R. Hawkins: Power vs. Force, p. 147, Hay House, 1995, 1998, 2004, 2012
23) Seka Nikolic: You Can Heal Yourself, p. 220, Pan Books, 2007
24) Anita Moorjani: Dying to Be Me, p. 132, Hay House, 2012, 2022
25) Dr. Joe Dispenza: Becoming Supernatural, p. 49, Hay House, Inc., 2017, 2019
26) David R. Hawkins: Letting Go, p. 15, Hay House, 2018
27) Kalliope Barlis: Phobia Relief, p. 30, Building Your Best Publications, 2016
28) Tim Ferriss: Tools of Titans, p. 137, Houghton Mifflin Harcourt, 2017
29) Bill Harris: Thresholds of the Mind, page 11, Centerpointe Press
30) Dr. John F. Demartini: The Breakthrough Experience™, p. 260, Hay House, 2002
31) David R. Hawkins: Transcending The Levels of Consciousness, p. 38, Hay House, 2006

Chapter Nine
1) David R. Hawkins: The Eye of the I, p. 79, Hay House, 2001
2) Paul McKenna: The 3 Things That Will Change Your Destiny Today, p. 122, Bantam Press, 2015

3) Richard Bandler, Alessio Roberti & Owen Fitzpatrick: How to Take Charge of Your Life, page 40, HarperCollins*Publishers*, 2014

4) Mihaly Csikszentmihalyi: Flow, The Classic Work on How to Achieve Happiness, p. 2, Rider, 2002

5) Bill Harris: Life Principles Integration Process, Course 2, Lesson 10, Paragraph 67

6) Esther and Jerry Hicks: Money and the Law of Attraction, p. 66, Hay House, 2008

7) David R. Hawkins: The Eye of the I, p. 219, Hay House, 2001

8) Lauri Järvilehto: Tee itsestäsi mestariajattelija, page 186, Kustannusosakeyhtiö Tammi, 2012

9) Michael Neill: Feel Happy Now!, page 57, Hay House, 2007

10) Tina Turner: Happiness Becomes You, p. 70, Astra Books, 2020

11) Deepak Chopra and Rudolph E. Tanzi: Super Genes, p. 208, Harmony Books, 2015

12) Robert Anton Wilson: Cosmic Trigger I, p. 89, New Falcon Publications 1977, 2013

13) Frank Martela: Valonöörit, p. 260, Gummerrus Kustannus Oy, 2015

14) Robert Anton Wilson: Cosmic Trigger I, p. 90, New Falcon Publications 1977, 2013

15) Syd Banks: Second Chance, p. 26, Fawcett Columbine, 1983, 1987

16) Richard Bandler & Garner Thomson: The Secrets of Being Happy, p. 258, I.M. Press, Inc.

17) Frank Martela: Valonöörit, p. 170, Gummerrus Kustannus Oy, 2015

18) Phil Jackson and Hugh Delehanty: Eleven Rings, The Penguin Press, 2013

Chapter Ten

1) Deepak Chopra: The Seven Spiritual Laws of Success, page 2, Amber-Allen Publishing and New World Library

2) Esther and Jerry Hicks: Ask and It Is Given, p. 276, Hay House, 2004, 2005, 2008

3) David R. Hawkins: Letting Go, p. 293, Hay House, 2018
4) Wayne W. Dyer: Manifest Your Soul's Purpose, Day 5, 27.07 min.
5) Simon Sinek: Start with Why, p. 86, Penguin Business, 2009
6) jackcanfield.com, The #1 reason you can't get what you want, 30.4.2015
7) Deepak Chopra and Rudolph E. Tanzi: Super Genes, p. 174, Harmony Books, 2015
8) Napoleon Hill: Think and Grow Rich, page 193, Jeremy P. Tarcher/Penguin (Your Magic Power to Be Rich)
9) David R. Hawkins: Power vs. Force, p. 225, Hay House, 1995, 1998, 2004, 2012
10) Jessica Huie: Purpose, p. 39, Hay House, 2018
11) Esther and Jerry Hicks: Ask and It Is Given, p. 102, Hay House, 2004, 2005, 2008
12) Stephen R. Covey: The 7 Habits of Highly Effective People, p. 105, Simon & Schuster, 1989, 2004
13) Dean Graziosi: Millionaire Success habits, p. 196, Growth Publishing, 2017
14) Paul McKenna: Change Your Life in Seven Days, page 112, Bantam Press, 2004
15) David R. Hawkins: Power vs. Force, p. 220, Hay House, 1995, 1998, 2004, 2012

Chapter Eleven

1) Raymond Holliwell: Working with the Law, p. v, LifeSuccess Productions, 1964, 2007
2) David R. Hawkins: Power vs. Force, p. 257, Hay House, 1995, 1998, 2004, 2012
3) Sandra Ingerman & Hank Wesselman: Awakening to the Spirit World, p. 216, Sounds True, 2010
4) Bill Harris: Thresholds of the Mind, page 43, Centerpointe Press

5) Napoleon Hill: Think and Grow Rich, p. 68, Your Magic Power to Be Rich, Penguin Books Ltd.

6) Richard Bandler, Alessio Roberti and Owen Fitzpatrick: The Ultimate Introduction to NLP, page 17, HarperCollins *Publishers*, 2015

7) Lars-Eric Uneståhl: Unestahl Mental Training®, Introduction 3/37

8) Dr. Joe Dispenza: Becoming Supernatural, p. 224, Hay House, Inc., 2017, 2019

9) Richard Bandler: Guide to Tranceformation, page 299, Health Communications, Inc., 2008

10) Jari Sarasvuo: Sisäinen sankari, s. 62, WSOY 1996.

11) Richard Branson: The Virgin Way, p. 2, Virgin Books, 2015

12) Lee Cockerell: Creating Magic, p. 140, Doubleday, 2008

13) Jack Canfield, Mark Victor Hansen & Amy Newmark: Chicken Soup for the Soul (20th Anniversary Edition), p. 204, Chicken Soup for the Soul Publishing, 2013

14) Esther and Jerry Hicks: Ask and It Is Given, p. 96, Hay House, 2004, 2005, 2008

15) Richard Bandler & Garner Thomson: The Secrets of Being Happy, p. 257, I.M. Press, Inc.

16) Dr. John F. Demartini: The Breakthrough Experience™, p. 2, Hay House, 2002

17) Michael Neill: You Can Have What You Want, page 50, Hay House, 2009

18) Joseph Murphy: The Power of Your Subconscious Mind, page 17, Prentice Hall Press, 2008

19) Jari Sarasvuo: Sisäinen sankari, s. 15, WSOY 1996.

20) - Richard Bandler: Guide to Tranceformation, page 122, Health Communications, Inc., 2008

21) Bruce H. Lipton: The Biology of Belief, p. 158, Hay House, 2015

22) David R. Hawkins: Letting Go, p. 15, Hay House, 2018

23) Anita Moorjani: Dying to Be Me, p. 153-154, Hay House, 2012, 2022
24) Richard Bandler, Alessio Roberti & Owen Fitzpatrick: How to Take Charge of Your Life, page 15, HarperCollins*Publishers*, 2014
25) Roxie Nafousi: Manifest, p. 83, Penguin Random House, 2022
26) Kay Cooke: Inspirations for Thriving Through Chaos, p. 40, Happy Brain Co Ltd, 2022
27) David R. Hawkins: Letting Go, p. xix, Hay House, 2018
28) Dean Graziosi: Millionaire Success habits, p. 196, Growth Publishing, 2017
29) Phil Jackson and Hugh Delehanty: Eleven Rings, p. 200, The Penguin Press, 2013
30) David R. Hawkins: The Eye of the I, p. 194-195, Hay House, 2001
31) Steve Lukather: The gospel According to Luke, p. x, Post Hill Press, 2019
32) Anita Moorjani: Dying to Be Me, p. 203, Hay House, 2012, 2022

Chapter Twelve

1) Dr. John F. Demartini: The Breakthrough Experience[TM], p. 35, Hay House, 2002
2) Paul McKenna: I Can Make you Happy, page 182, Bantam Press, 2011
3) Roxie Nafousi: Manifest, p. 111, Penguin Random House, 2022
4) Tim Ferriss: Tools of Titans, p. 399, Houghton Mifflin Harcourt, 2017
5) Dr. John F. Demartini: The Breakthrough Experience[TM], p. 5, Hay House, 2002
6) Jack Canfield, Mark Victor Hansen & Amy Newmark: Chicken Soup for the Soul (20th Anniversary Edition), p. 315, Chicken Soup for the Soul Publishing, 2013
7) Dr. John F. Demartini: The Breakthrough Experience[TM], p. 12, Hay House, 2002
8) Roxie Nafousi: Manifest, p. 118, Penguin Random House, 2022

9) Dr. John F. Demartini: The Breakthrough Experience™, p. 6, Hay House, 2002

Chapter Thirteen

1) David R. Hawkins: Letting Go, p. 19, Hay House, 2018
2) Roxie Nafousi: Manifest, p. 37, Penguin Random House, 2022
3) Richard Bach: Illusions, p. 114, Arrow Books, 1977
4) Dr Richard Bandler & Owen Fitzpatrick: Memories. Hope is the Question, p. 68, Mysterious Publications, 2014
5) Ulla Suokko: Signs of the Universe, p.7, WiseWoman, 2020
6) Michael Neill: The Inside Out Revolution, page 59, Hay House
7) Roxie Nafousi: Manifest, p. 51, Penguin Random House, 2022
8) David R. Hawkins: Letting Go, p. 112, Hay House, 2018

Chapter Fourteen

1) Richard Bandler, Alessio Roberti & Owen Fitzpatrick: How to Take Charge of Your Life, page 12, HarperCollins*Publishers*, 2014
2) Esther and Jerry Hicks: Money and the Law of Attraction, p. 180-181, Hay House, 2008
3) Viktor E. Frankl: Man's Search for Meaning, p. 66, Beacon Press, 2006
4) Owen Fitzpatrick: Conversations with Richard Bandler, page 50, Health Communications, Inc.
5) Moshe Feldenkrais: The Master Moves, p. 20, Meta Publications, 1984
6) Viktor E. Frankl: Man's Search for Meaning, p. X, Beacon Press, 2006
7) Tina Turner: Happiness Becomes You, p. 82, Astra Books, 2020
8) Brendon Burchard: The Motivation Manifesto, page 18, Hay House, Inc, 2014
9) Alberto Villodo: Revolutionary Healing Techniques from the Ancient Shamans, Hay House Heal Summit, Day 5, 54 min., 2021

10) David R. Hawkins: Power vs. Force, p. 123, Hay House, 1995, 1998, 2004, 2012
11) Dr. John F. Demartini: The Breakthrough Experience™, p. 126, Hay House, 2002
12) Kay Cooke: Inspirations for Thriving Through Chaos, p. 234, Happy Brain Co Ltd, 2022

Chapter Fifteen

1) Ulla Suokko: Signs of the Universe, p.163, WiseWoman, 2020
2) Dr. John F. Demartini: The Breakthrough Experience™, p. 32, Hay House, 2002
3) Syd Banks: Second Chance, p. 85-86, Fawcett Columbine, 1983, 1987
4) David R. Hawkins: The Eye of the I, p. 328, Hay House, 2001
5) Ulla Suokko: Signs of the Universe, p.97-98, WiseWoman, 2020
6) Anita Moorjani: Dying to Be Me, p. 172, Hay House, 2012, 2022
7) Roxie Nafousi: Manifest, p. 51, Penguin Random House, 2022
8) Tina Turner: Happiness Becomes You, p. 123, Astra Books, 2020
9) Ulla Suokko: Signs of the Universe, p.162-163, WiseWoman, 2020
10) Anita Moorjani: Dying to Be Me, p. 185, Hay House, 2012, 2022
11) Roxie Nafousi: Manifest, p. 51, Penguin Random House, 2022
12) Anita Moorjani: Dying to Be Me, p. 204, Hay House, 2012, 2022
13) Dr. John F. Demartini: The Breakthrough Experience™, p. 15, Hay House, 2002
14) Dr. Richard Bandler, as heard in many of his seminars
15) Anita Moorjani: Dying to Be Me, p. 206, Hay House, 2012, 2022
16) Anita Moorjani: Dying to Be Me, p. 206, Hay House, 2012, 2022
17) David R. Hawkins: The Eye of the I, p. 82z, Hay House, 2001
18) Phil Jackson and Hugh Delehanty: Eleven Rings, p. 4, The Penguin Press, 2013
19) Michael Neill: You Can Have What You Want, page 4, Hay House

20) David R. Hawkins: Power vs. Force, p. 312, Hay House, 1995, 1998, 2004, 2012

21) Anita Moorjani: Dying to Be Me, p. 185, Hay House, 2012, 2022

22) Michael Neill: You Can Have What You Want, page 24, Hay House

Chapter Sixteen

1) Seka Nikolic: You Can Heal Yourself, p. 182, Pan Books, 2007

2) David R. Hawkins: Power vs. Force, p. 230, Hay House, 1995, 1998, 2004, 2012

3) Bruce H. Lipton: The Biology of Belief, p. 137-138, Hay House, 2015

4) Dr. Joe Dispenza: Becoming Supernatural, p. 41, Hay House, Inc., 2017, 2019

5) Deepak Chopra and Rudolph E. Tanzi: Super Genes, p. 1, Harmony Books, 2015

6) Seka Nikolic: You Can Heal Yourself, p. 182, Pan Books, 2007

7) David R. Hawkins: Letting Go, p. 205, Hay House, 2018

8) Lauri Nummenmaa: Tunnekartasto, p.256, Kustannusosakeyhtiö Tammi, 2019

9) Paul McKenna: The 3 Things That Will Change Your Destiny Today, p. 62, Bantam Press, 2015

10) Esther and Jerry Hicks: Money and the Law of Attraction, p. 99, Hay House, 2008

11) Anita Moorjani: Dying to Be Me, p. 117, Hay House, 2012, 2022

12) Bruce H. Lipton: The Biology of Belief, p. 140, Hay House, 2015

13) David R. Hawkins: Letting Go, p. 16, Hay House, 2018

14) Deepak Chopra and Rudolph E. Tanzi: Super Genes, p. 20, Harmony Books, 2015

15) Seka Nikolic: You Can Heal Yourself, p. 181, Pan Books, 2007

16) Michael Neill: Feel Happy Now!, page 128-129, Hay House, 2007

17) Lauri Nummenmaa: Tunnekartasto, p.57, Kustannusosakeyhtiö Tammi, 2019

18) Deepak Chopra and Rudolph E. Tanzi: Super Genes, p. 220, Harmony Books, 2015
19) Seka Nikolic: You Can Heal Yourself, p. 181, Pan Books, 2007
20) Lauri Järvilehto: Tee itsestäsi mestariajattelija, page 119, Kustannusosakeyhtiö Tammi, 2012
21) David R. Hawkins: The Eye of the I, p. 35, Hay House, 2001
22) Dr. Joe Dispenza: You Are the Placebo, p. 96, Hay House Inc., 2014
23) Seka Nikolic: You Can Heal Yourself, p. 220, Pan Books, 2007
24) Héctor Garcia and Francesc Miralles: Ikigai, p. 20, Penguin Random House, 2016
25) Dr. Wayne W. Dyer: Wishes Fulfilled, p. 25, Hay House, inc. 2012
26) Michael Talbot: The Holographic Universe, p. 117, HarperCollins*Publishers*, 1996
27) Nick Ortner: The Tapping Solution, p. 35, Hay House, Inc., 2013
28) David R. Hawkins: Power vs. Force, p. 233, Hay House, 1995, 1998, 2004, 2012

Chapter Seventeen

1) Anita Moorjani: Dying to Be Me, p. 159, Hay House, 2012, 2022
2) Richard Bach: Illusions, p. 110, Arrow Books, 1977
3) Paul McKenna: The 3 Things That Will Change Your Destiny Today, p. 18, Bantam Press, 2015
4) Stephen R. Covey: The 7 Habits of Highly Effective People, p. 366, Simon & Schuster, 1989, 2004
5) Michael Neill: Super Coach, p. 2, Hay House
6) Seka Nikolic: You Can Heal Yourself, p. 184, Pan Books, 2007
7) Bill Harris: The Secrets to Success and Making Money in Good Times or Bad, Lesson 19
8) Timothy Ferriss: The 4-Hour Body, p. 465, Carmenere On, LLC, 2010
9) Lauri Järvilehto: Tee itsestäsi mestariajattelija, page 57, Kustannusosakeyhtiö Tammi, 2012

10) Jack Canfield, Mark Victor Hansen & Amy Newmark: Chicken Soup for the Soul (20th Anniversary Edition), p. 245, Chicken Soup for the Soul Publishing, 2013

11) Bill Harris: The Life Principles Integration Process, Lesson 1, paragraph 110

12) Frank Martela: Valonöörit, p. 11-12, Gummerrus Kustannus Oy, 2015

13) Jack Canfield: The Success Principles™, p. 9, William Morrow, 2005

14) Napoleon Hill: Think and Grow Rich, page 139, Jeremy P. Tarcher/Penguin (Your Magic Power to Be Rich)

15) Jack Canfield, Mark Victor Hansen & Amy Newmark: Chicken Soup for the Soul (20th Anniversary Edition), p. 216, Chicken Soup for the Soul Publishing, 2013

16) Jack Canfield, Mark Victor Hansen & Amy Newmark: Chicken Soup for the Soul (20th Anniversary Edition), p. 266, Chicken Soup for the Soul Publishing, 2013

17) Dr Richard Bandler & Owen Fitzpatrick: Memories. Hope is the Question, p. 165, Mysterious Publications, 2014

18) W. Chan Kim & Renée Mauborgne: Blue Ocean Strategy, page 185, Harvard Business School Publishing Corporation, 2005

19) Lauri Järvilehto: Tee itsestäsi mestariajattelija, page 70, Kustannusosakeyhtiö Tammi, 2012

20) Richard Branson: The Virgin Way, p. 372-273, Virgin Books, 2015

21) Bill Harris: The Secrets to Success And Making Money, Module 1, Lesson 4 (at 3 minutes)

22) Napoleon Hill: The Magic Ladder to Success, page 299, Jeremy P. Tarcher/Penguin (Your Magic Power to Be Rich)

23) Paul McKenna: I Can Make You Thin, page 29, Transworld Publishers, 2010

24) Richard Bandler, Alessio Roberti & Owen Fitzpatrick: How to Take Charge of Your Life, page 88, HarperCollinsPublishers, 2014

25) Lauri Järvilehto: Tee itsestäsi mestariajattelija, page 204, Kustannusosakeyhtiö Tammi, 2012

26) Michael Neill: Feel Happy Now!, page 80, Hay House, 2007

27) Mihaly Csikszentmihalyi: Flow, The Classic Work on How to Achieve Happiness, p. 217, Rider, 2002

28) Esther and Jerry Hicks: Ask and It Is Given, p. xiv, Hay House, 2004, 2005, 2008

29) Esther and Jerry Hicks: Ask and It Is Given, p. 222, Hay House, 2004, 2005, 2008

30) Dr. Alexander Sinigoj: 7 Rituals of Self-Made Millionaires, p. 40

31) Esther and Jerry Hicks: Ask and It Is Given, p. 281, Hay House, 2004, 2005, 2008

32) Stephen R. Covey: The 7 Habits of Highly Effective People, p. 78, Simon & Schuster, 1989, 2004

33) Frank Martela: Valonöörit, p. 106, Gummerrus Kustannus Oy, 2015

34) Richard Bandler and Garner Thomson: The Secrets of Being Happy, p. 180, I.M. Press, Inc., 2011

35) Susan Jeffers: Feel The Fear and Do It Anyway, p. 71-72, Vermilion, 1987, 2007, 2012

36) Dr. John F. Demartini: The Breakthrough Experience™, p. 63, Hay House, 2002

37) John Assaraf: Having it All, p. 189, Atria Books

38) Deepak Chopra and Rudolph E. Tanzi: Super Genes, p. 99, Harmony Books, 2015

39) Anita Moorjani: Dying to Be Me, p. 147, Hay House, 2012, 2022

40) Tina Turner: Happiness Becomes You, p. 167, Astra Books, 2020

41) Christie Marie Sheldon: Unlimited Abundance, Lesson 14, Mindvalley.com

42) Simon Sinek: Start with Why, p. 66, Penguin Business, 2009

43) Roxie Nafousi: Manifest, p. 85, Penguin Random House, 2022

44) Susan Jeffers: Feel The Fear and Do It Anyway, p. 35, Vermilion, 1987, 2007, 2012

45) Richard Bandler, Alessio Roberti & Owen Fitzpatrick: How to Take Charge of Your Life, page 69, HarperCollinsPublishers, 2014

46) John Assaraf: Having it All, p. 112, Atria Books

47) Michael Neill: Feel Happy Now!, page 52, Hay House, 2007

48) Paul McKenna: "I Can Make you Happy", page 52, Bantam Press

49) Anthony Robbins: Awaken the Giant Within, p. 32, Free Press

50) Richard Bandler, Alessio Roberti and Owen Fitzpatrick: The Ultimate Introduction to NLP, page 125, HarperCollins Publishers, 2013

51) Joe Vitale: The Attractor Factor, page 232, John Wiley & Sons, Inc.

52) Richard Bandler and John Grinder: Reframing, p. 96, Real People Press, 1982

53) David R. Hawkins: The Eye of the I, p. 268, Hay House, 2001

54) Steven J. Stowell & Matt M. Starcevich: The Coach, p. 17, The Center for Management and Organization Effectiveness, 1987, 1998

55) Michael Neill: Super Coach, p. 102, Hay House

56) Dr. Richard Bandler & Owen Fitzpatrick: Thinking on Purpose, p. 81, New Thinking Publications, 2019

57) Richard Bandler, John La Valle, Anders Piper, Alessio Roberti, Alessandro Mora, Kate Benson, Garner Thomson, Owen Fitzpatrick: Seven Practical Applications of NLP, p. 49, Attrakt BV, 2012

58) Anita Moorjani: Dying to Be Me, p. 117, Hay House, 2012, 2022

59) David R. Hawkins: Power vs. Force, p. 223, Hay House, 1995, 1998, 2004, 2012

Chapter Eighteen

1) Kalliope Barlis: Phobia Relief, p. 22, Building Your Best Publications, 2016

2) Richard Bandler, Alessio Roberti & Owen Fitzpatrick: How to Take Charge of Your Life, page 122, HarperCollins*Publishers*, 2014

3) Dr. John F. Demartini: The Breakthrough Experience™, p. xii, Hay House, 2002
4) Dr. Joe Dispenza: Becoming Supernatural, p. 46, Hay House, Inc., 2017, 2019
5) Owen Fitzpatrick: The Charismatic Edge, p. 21, Gill Books, 2013
6) Michael Neill: The Inside Out Revolution, page 40, Hay House
7) Joseph Murphy: The Power of Your Subconscious Mind, page 227-228, Prentice Hall Press
8) Michael Neill: The Inside Out Revolution, page 25, Hay House

Chapter Nineteen

1) Joe Vitale: Hypnotic Writing, p. 153, John Wiley & Sons, Inc., 2007
2) Rhonda Byrne: The Power, page 40, Simon & Schuster OK Ltd.
3) Jack Canfield, Mark Victor Hansen & Amy Newmark: Chicken Soup for the Soul (20th Anniversary Edition), p. 318, Chicken Soup for the Soul Publishing, 2013
4) Lauri Järvilehto: Tee itsestäsi mestariajattelija, page 67, Kustannusosakeyhtiö Tammi, 2012
5) Jari Litmanen: Litmanen10, page 282, Kustannusosakeyhtiö Tammi, 2015
6) Richard Bandler, Alessio Roberti & Owen Fitzpatrick: How to Take Charge of Your Life, page 4, HarperCollins*Publishers*, 2014
7) Bruce H. Lipton: The Biology of Belief, p. xxv, Hay House, 2015
8) Bill Harris: Thresholds of the Mind, page 128, Centerpointe Press
9) Mihaly Csikszentmihalyi: Flow, The Classic Work on How to Achieve Happiness, p. 48, Rider, 2002
10) Viktor E. Frankl: Man's Search for Meaning, p. 67, Beacon Press, 2006
11) Kalliope Barlis: Phobia Relief, p. 23-24, Building Your Best Publications, 2016

12) Richard Bandler, Alessio Roberti & Owen Fitzpatrick: How to Take Charge of Your Life, page 117, HarperCollins*Publishers*, 2014
13) Anthony Robbins: Awaken the Giant Within, p. 32-33, Free Press
14) James Kingsland: Siddhartha's Brain, p. 244, HarperCollins Publishers, 2016
15) Richard Bandler: Using Your Brain for a Change, p. 42, Real People Press, 1985
16) Mihaly Csikszentmihalyi: Flow, The Classic Work on How to Achieve Happiness, p. 191, Rider, 2002
17) Anita Moorjani: Dying to Be Me, p. 201-202, Hay House, 2012, 2022
18) Michael Neill: The Inside Out Revolution, page 81, Hay House
19) Frank Martela: Valonöörit, p. 259, Gummerrus Kustannus Oy, 2015

Chapter Twenty

1) David R. Hawkins: The Eye of the I, p. 413, Hay House, 2001
2) https://youtu.be/vg-D2DMFbhk?si=I2EOJu3r5aTF-c7u

Bibliography

John Assaraf: Having it All, Atria Books, 2007

Richard Bach: Illusions, Arrow Books, 1977

Dan S. Bagley III and Edward J. Reese: Beyond Selling, Meta Publications, 1988

Richard Bandler: Get the Life You Want, HarperElement, 2008

Richard Bandler: Guide to Tranceformation, Health Communications, Inc., 2008

Richard Bandler: Using Your Brain for a Change, Real People Press, 1985

Richard Bandler & Owen Fitzpatrick: Conversations with Richard Bandler, Health Communications, Inc. 2009

Dr Richard Bandler & Owen Fitzpatrick: Memories. Hope is the Question, Mysterious Publications, 2014

Richard Bandler and Owen Fitzpatrick: Patterns for Problem Solving, NLP Tranceformations inc., 2022

Dr. Richard Bandler & Owen Fitzpatrick: Thinking on Purpose, New Thinking Publications, 2019

Richard Bandler and John Grinder: Reframing, Real People Press, 1982

Richard Bandler & John La Valle: Persuasion Engineering™, Meta Publications Inc., 1996

Richard Bandler, John La Valle, Anders Piper, Alessio Roberti, Alessandro Mora, Kate Benson, Garner Thomson, Owen Fitzpatrick: Seven Practical Applications of NLP, Attrakt BV, 2012

Richard Bandler, Alessio Roberti & Owen Fitzpatrick: How to Take Charge of Your Life, HarperCollins*Publishers*, 2014

Richard Bandler, Alessio Roberti and Owen Fitzpatrick: The Ultimate Introduction to NLP, HarperCollins *Publishers*, 2013

Richard Bandler & Garner Thomson: The Secrets of Being Happy, I.M. Press, Inc., 2011

Syd Banks: Second Chance, Fawcett Columbine, 1983, 1987

Kalliope Barlis: Phobia Relief, Building Your Best Publications, 2016

Richard Branson: The Virgin Way, Virgin Books, 2015

Derren Brown: Tricks of the Mind, Transworld Publishers, 2007

Brendon Burchard: The Motivation Manifesto, Hay House, Inc, 2014

Rhonda Byrne: The Power, Simon & Schuster OK Ltd., 2010

Jack Canfield: The Success Principles™, William Morrow, 2005

Jack Canfield, Mark Victor Hansen & Amy Newmark: Chicken Soup for the Soul (20th Anniversary Edition), Chicken Soup for the Soul Publishing, 2013

Carlos Castaneda: The Fire from Within, Touchstone Books, 1998

Deepak Chopra: The Seven Spiritual Laws of Success, Amber-Allen Publishing and New World Library, 1994

Deepak Chopra and Rudolph E. Tanzi: Super Genes, Harmony Books, 2015

Lee Cockerell: Creating Magic, Doubleday, 2008

Kay Cooke: Inspirations for Thriving Through Chaos, Happy Brain Co Ltd, 2022

Stephen R. Covey: The 7 Habits of Highly Effective People, Simon & Schuster, 1989, 2004

Mihaly Csikszentmihalyi: Flow, The Classic Work on How to Achieve Happiness, Rider, 2002

Dr. John F. Demartini: The Breakthrough Experience™, Hay House, 2002

Robert Dilts: Changing Belief Systems with NLP, Meta Publications, 1990

Robert Dilts, Tim Hallbom and Suzi Smith: Beliefs, Crown House Publishing Ltd, 2012

Dr. Joe Dispenza: Becoming Supernatural, Hay House, Inc., 2017, 2019

Dr. Joe Dispenza: You Are the Placebo, Hay House Inc., 2014

Dr. Wayne W. Dyer: Wishes Fulfilled, Hay House, inc. 2012

Moshe Feldenkrais: The Master Moves, Meta Publications, 1984

Timothy Ferriss: The 4-Hour Body, Carmenere On, LLC, 2010

Tim Ferriss: Tools of Titans, Houghton Mifflin Harcourt, 2017

Owen Fitzpatrick: The Charismatic Edge, Gill Books, 2013

Viktor E. Frankl: Man's Search for Meaning, Beacon Press, 2006

Héctor Garcia and Francesc Miralles: Ikigai, Penguin Random House, 2016

Michael S. Gazzaniga: Who's in Charge?, Robinson, 2016

Dean Graziosi: Millionaire Success habits, Growth Publishing, 2017

Bill Harris: Thresholds of the Mind, Centerpointe Press, 2007

David R. Hawkins: Letting Go, Hay House, 2018

David R. Hawkins: Power vs. Force, Hay House, 1995, 1998, 2004, 2012

David R. Hawkins: The Eye of the I, Hay House, 2001

David R. Hawkins: Transcending The Levels of Consciousness, Hay House, 2006

Esther and Jerry Hicks: Ask and It Is Given, Hay House, 2004, 2005, 2008

Esther and Jerry Hicks: Money and the Law of Attraction, Hay House, 2008

Napoleon Hill: The Magic Ladder to Success, Jeremy P. Tarcher/Penguin (Your Magic Power to Be Rich), 1930, 2007

Napoleon Hill: The Master-Key to Riches, Penguin Books Ltd./JMW Group Inc., 1945, 2007

Napoleon Hill: Think and Grow Rich, Jeremy P. Tarcher/Penguin (Your Magic Power to Be Rich), 1937, 2005

Raymond Holliwell: Working with the Law, LifeSuccess Productions, 1964, 2007

Jessica Huie: Purpose, Hay House, 2018

Sandra Ingerman & Hank Wesselman: Awakening to the Spirit World, Sounds True, 2010

Phil Jackson and Hugh Delehanty: Eleven Rings, The Penguin Press, 2013

Susan Jeffers: Feel The Fear and Do It Anyway, Vermilion, 1987, 2007, 2012

Lauri Järvilehto: Tee itsestäsi mestariajattelija, Kustannusosakeyhtiö Tammi, 2012

W. Chan Kim & Renée Mauborgne: Blue Ocean Strategy, Harvard Business School Publishing Corporation, 2005

James Kingsland: Siddhartha's Brain, HarperCollins Publishers, 2016

Rob Kosberg: Publish. Promote. Profit™., 2018

Bruce H. Lipton: The Biology of Belief, Hay House, 2015

Jari Litmanen: Litmanen10, Kustannusosakeyhtiö Tammi, 2015

Steve Lukather: The Gospel According to Luke, Post Hill Press, 2019

Frank Martela: Valonöörit, Gummerrus Kustannus Oy, 2015

Paul McKenna: Change Your Life in Seven Days, Bantam Press, 2004

Paul McKenna: I Can Make you Happy, Bantam Press, 2011

Paul McKenna: I Can Make You Thin, Transworld Publishers, 2010

Paul McKenna: Instant Influence & Charisma, Bantam Press, 2015

Paul McKenna: The 3 Things That Will Change Your Destiny Today, Bantam Press, 2015

Jillian Michaels: Unlimited, Three Rivers Press, 2011

Anita Moorjani: Dying to Be Me, Hay House, 2012, 2022

Joseph Murphy: The Power of Your Subconscious Mind, Prentice Hall Press, 2008

Roxie Nafousi: Manifest, Penguin Random House, 2022

Michael Neill: Feel Happy Now!, Hay House, 2007

Michael Neill: Super Coach, Hay House, 2009

Michael Neill: The Inside Out Revolution, Hay House, 2013

Michael Neill: You Can Have What You Want, Hay House, 2009

Seka Nikolic: You Can Heal Yourself, Pan Books, 2007

Lauri Nummenmaa: Tunnekartasto, Kustannusosakeyhtiö Tammi, 2019

Nick Ortner: The Tapping Solution, Hay House, Inc., 2013

David Perlmutter and Alberto Villoldo: Power Up Your Brain, Hay House, 2011

Anthony Robbins: Awaken the Giant Within, Free Press, 2003

Tony Robbins: Money: Master The Game, Simon & Schuster, 2014

Jari Sarasvuo: Sisäinen sankari, WSOY 1996.

Simon Sinek: Start with Why, Penguin Business, 2009

Anik Singal: The Circle of Profit, Lurn Inc., 2016

Dr. Alexander Sinigoj: 7 Rituals of Self-Made Millionaires,

Jamie Smart: The Little Book of Clarity, Capstone, 2015

Bobbe Sommer and Maxwell Maltz: Psycho-cybernetics 2000, Prentice Hall Press, 2000

Steven J. Stowell & Matt M. Starcevich: The Coach, The Center for Management and Organization Effectiveness, 1987, 1998

Ulla Suokko: Signs of the Universe, WiseWoman, 2020

Michael Talbot: The Holographic Universe, HarperCollins*Publishers*, 1996

Tina Turner: Happiness Becomes You, Astra Books, 2020

Joe Vitale: The Attractor Factor, John Wiley & Sons, Inc.

Joe Vitale: Hypnotic Writing, John Wiley & Sons, Inc., 2007

Joe Vitale: Zero Limits, John Wiley & Sons Inc. 2007

Alan Watts: The Essential Alan Watts, Transformational Book Circle, 2006

Robert Anton Wilson: Cosmic Trigger I, New Falcon Publications 1977, 2013

Robert Anton Wilson: Cosmic Trigger II – Down to Earth, New Falcon Publications, 1995

Robert Anton Wilson: Prometheus Rising, Hilaritas Press, 1983

Robert Anton Wilson: Quantum Psychology, New Falcon Publications, 1990

Michael D. Yapko: Essentials of Hypnosis, Routledge, 2015

About The Author

Hannu Pirilä is one of Finland's leading NLP trainers and self-development coaches. He is known for the books he has written, his results-producing coaching, and the Your Own Blue Ocean coaching concept he has developed, all of which have resulted in a significantly better quality of life and mental well-being for innumerous people.

Hannu's background is in managerial and leadership positions in the hotel and restaurant industry, where his more than 15-year career included jobs not only in Finland but also in Switzerland, Luxembourg, Russia, China and the USA.

In 2004, Hannu left from the operational world of the hotel and restaurant industry and moved to consulting for companies in the hotel and restaurant industry and various service sectors, working also some time in sales and sales management.

In 2008, Hannu joined a company specializing in international hotel consulting as a hotel consultant and about a year later founded his own consulting and training company. Around the same time, Hannu also began seriously studying NLP, completing several NLP certificates and licenses in a short time. Today, Hannu is an internationally respected Licensed Master Trainer of NLP™ who works also in the team of assisting NLP Trainers in the seminars of NLP co-founder Dr. Richard Bandler and world-famous hypnotist Paul McKenna.

Paul McKenna and his team of assistant trainers in London 5/2016. Hannu is second from the right, Paul McKenna fifth from the right.

Hannu is the CEO and owner of HPA Consulting Oy, which he founded in 2009. He has completed e.g. eMBA (executive Master of Business Administration) and BSc degrees and he is a business management expert accredited by the IIB (Institute for Independent Business International) and a member of the board of LAK Business Experts in 2012-2016.

Hannu's certifications:

- Licensed Master Trainer of NLP™ for Business (2023)
- Licensed NLP Coaching Trainer™ (2022)
- Licensed Trainer of NLP® (2011, 2013, 2015, 2018, 2022)
- Licensed Master Practitioner of NLP® (2010)
- Licensed Practitioner of NLP® (2010)
- Licensed NLP Coach™ (2010)
- Licensed Business Master Practitioner of NLP™ (2015)

- Licensed Business Practitioner of NLP™ (2010)
- Licensed LAB Profile™ Practitioner (2010)
- Persuasion Engineering® (2012)
- Licensed Sports Performance Coach™ (2011)
- Licensed Specialist Practitioner of Neuro-Hypnotic Repatterning™ (2013), Level 2 (2023)
- Design Human Engineer™ (2017), Level 2 (2020), Level 3 (2022)
- Henkinen Valmentaja® (Mental Coach) (2013)
- Clinical Hypnotherapist (2020)

In addition to working as an NLP trainer and an NLP coach, Hannu also works as a personal growth coach, a mental coach for athletes and a speaker at seminars and other events.

On the corporate side, he has consulted both individual entrepreneurs and listed companies. On the sports side, he has worked as a mental coach for both junior basketball players and professional soccer players, as well as amateur tennis players and world champions in MMA. In addition to this, Hannu has helped numerous people from all walks of life, e.g. to get help for the fear of flying, stop smoking, lose weight and make other significant changes to improve their quality of life.

Hannu has written the popular books *Your Own Blue Ocean, Better life and NLP* and *The Little Book of Personal-Development, Success and Happiness*.

Hannu has studied under such world-renowned personal development masters as Dr. Richard Bandler, John La Valle, Kathleen La Valle, Bill Harris, Paul McKenna, and Bob Proctor.

Hannu is an avid sports and physical exercise enthusiast. He has played semi-professionally basketball and has additionally competed on different amateur levels in volleyball, tennis and martial arts. Hannu holds black belts in taekwondo and hapkido and does strength training on a regular basis.

The best way to contact Hannu is by e-mail at hannu@hannupirila.com or via his website www.hannupirila.com.

Other Books by Hannu Pirilä

Your Own Blue Ocean

Practical advice and exercises for defining and achieving your own success, enhancing your sense of happiness and finding Your Own Blue Ocean

"A book that gives you, the reader, the tools to change the very direction of your life. While many of the tools here come from my work, the package of how Hannu has assembled them is both unique and delightful. He has kept the simplicity I have always striven for and also presented a package for the reader to learn how to look beyond their own limitation to the very horizon of possibility."

-Dr. Richard Bandler,
Co-founder of NLP, author of more than 30 books and creator of behavioral technologies

Your Own Blue Ocean is a guide for people to get the new life they want – no matter where they are in their life at the moment.

Your Own Blue Ocean is not, however, a mundane or conventional guide for a better life. This book does not contain any new age hype or forced happiness exercises. Your Own Blue Ocean is a tried and proven method that propels you toward a new life you want, designed by yourself.

This book will not tell you what to do. Rather, through the included instructions and exercises, you can find a new course for your life, and thereby the best means, to find and achieve Your Own Blue Ocean.

Available on Amazon and other internet bookstores.

Better Life and NLP

Inspirational ideas and practical guidelines for NLP, mind control, mental well-being, self-management and better life

Hannu Pirilä

Better Life and NLP

Inspirational ideas and practical guidelines for NLP, mental well-being, self-leadership and better life

How to better control your own thinking and thereby change your actions and behavior?

How to improve your quality of life and achieve better results in life?

Our quality of life is formed by what meaning we give to things in our life, what kind of choices we make and how we act and behave in different situations. By controlling our thinking and mind, we also control our behavior and the meaning we give to something.

This book contains ideas, instructions and techniques for life management and self-leadership. The different chapters of the book introduce the reader to the use of Neuro-Linguistic Programming, NLP, through different topics.

This book won't tell you what you should think or how you should act, because it all depends on your own goals and what you value. Instead, this book will tell you how you can make the changes you want in your own thinking and, through that, bring about concrete changes to improve your own quality of life.

Available on Amazon and other internet bookstores.

The Little Book of Personal Development, Success and Happiness

A little book that provides helpful ideas to help you gain insights and ideas for a better and happier life and success.

As the title implies, this book discusses the significance of personal development as a key factor in success and happiness.

The book is a collection of the most important and useful thoughts and ideas of the author, which will help you to get new insights and make your life better and happier. Since this book in intended to be as comprehensible and easy to read as possible, the thoughts and ideas have been expressed in a compressed form, leaving space for you as a reader to generate your own opinions on things. The book will give you an abundance of ideas and inspiration to go out and explore your own path on your self-development.

Self-development is a lifelong journey that requires constant learning and openness to new thoughts and ideas. The goal of the book is to give you the nudge you need to figure out what you really want, what your passion is, and that you will achieve the success and happiness that awaits for you and that belongs to you.

This second edition of the book has been updated with some minor changes to the chapters that existed already in the first edition. Moreover, there are now two whole new chapters in this edition to provide even more insights and ideas.

Available on Amazon and other internet bookstores.